ENJOYING PERTHSHIRE

Campbell Steven

———————

Poems by Kenneth C. Steven

———————

Perth & Kinross District Libraries
1994

BY THE SAME AUTHOR

The Island Hills

Scotland
(*Panorama-Books Series*)

The Central Highlands
(*Scottish Mountaineering Club Guide Book*)

Glens and Straths of Scotland

Enjoying Scotland
(*Foyle's Travel Book Club Choice*)

The Story of Scotland's Hills

Proud Record
(*The Story of the Glasgow Fire Service*)

An Anthology of Hope

————————

BY KENNETH C. STEVEN

Fiction: The Unborn
Dan

Poetry Collections: Remembering Peter
The Pearl Fisher

————————

Enjoying Perthshire Published by Perth & Kinross District Libraries

ISBN No. 0905452 17 8

Printed by Sunprint, 38 Tay Street, Perth and Upper Craigs, Stirling.

Ben A'an (1750 feet) on the eastern edge of the Trossachs.

FOREWORD

One of the great satisfactions of Scotland is its variety. There can be very few places on earth where so many variations of scenery are crowded into so small a space and where so many areas are rich with their own character and characteristics. The Cairngorms would look strange in Argyll, and the Borders are not likely to be mistaken for Sutherland, while Perthshire is as individualistic as any.

To me all the areas of Scotland are like old and comfortable friends, loved for themselves, to be greeted and enjoyed, to be left with fond memories and the faith of "being there" in our hearts for ever. Perthshire is a very old friend — with a worthy advocate in Campbell Steven. His books have long been appreciated: *The Island Hills, Glens and Straths of Scotland, Enjoying Scotland, The Story of Scotland's Hills* among them.

This is not a guidebook in a dull step-by-step directive way, but a survey and personal narration by someone who has explored in the best sense, and wishes to share the good experiences. We are given stories and ideas about hill-walking, cycling, bird-watching, waterfall exploration, following an old military road; we are helped with Gaelic names and given apposite quotes from other travellers. There is the richness of son Kenneth's poems and all the complementary illustrations. As Campbell joined the Scottish Mountaineering Club the year I was born, 1934, we have a long distillation to savour. Here is someone who has certainly enjoyed a very special part of Scotland.

Perthshire uniquely marches with *nine* other counties, which emphasises just how central it is. Dominated by the River Tay and its tributaries, these glens and straths (Glen Lyon is the longest glen in Scotland) have been its history. The A9 is a major artery in the body of Scotland. The varied geology has given rich greens as well as the hues of moor and mountain, and a goodly share of major lochs. In the old droving days, the cattle of the Highlands and Islands converged through the county to Crieff and the Lowlands. Now we go "by Tummel and by Rannoch" of the song, for pleasure and recreation.

Standing on top of the Round Tower at Abernethy with its historical associations, gazing over Rannoch Moor from Rannoch Station, resting on top of the county (Ben Lawers, ninth highest summit in Britain), following a shady walk up to the Hermitage, or chatting into the Festival Theatre at Pitlochry after dinner are all Perthshire experiences. We sometimes forget just how big Perthshire is as well as how varied.

Let me tell you a personal story about that incomparable theatre. When still at school under the Ochils (only a few miles outwith Perthshire!) I cycled to the then new tent-in-the-hills theatre and arrived in a deluge. A kind member of staff, a Mr Stewart, took pity on me and showed me round and then treated me to supper. Later I realised he was the theatre's founder. That night I slept in a haystack, richly rewarded — and I've been back and back every year since. That is the way to make friends, and Perthshire is good at welcoming the visitor. Whether you are a first-time arrival or a golden oldie, this is the book to carry with you when enjoying Perthshire.

Hamish M. Brown

CONTENTS

———————

Introduction

1	Enjoying Ways on the Hills	High View Schiehallion	9
2	Enjoying Cycling down the Map	Song: The Empty Glens Glen Lyon	21
3	Enjoying a Century of Birds	Voices Sighting	35
4	Enjoying the Woods and the Trees	The Motorway Forest The Chestnut Days	47
5	Enjoying a Wade Road	Wayside Encounter – Highland Bull Heather Track	59
6	Enjoying Waterfall Days	The Camp The Linn	71
7	Enjoying Family "Five-milers"	For Life Itself Once Before	85

Illustrations

Ben A'an (1750 feet) on the eastern edge of the Trossachs — 2

Schiehallion from the east, beyond Loch Kinardochy — 11

Ben More and Stobinian from near Crianlarich — 13

Lochan nan Cat and An Stuc, a subsidiary "top" of Ben Lawers — 14

Snow-patches and sunshine at the top of Ben Vrackie — 15

At the top of Central Gully near the summit of Beinn Laoigh — 17

The quaich and aneroid which belonged to the Perthshire Mountain Club — 18

A familiar view of Schiehallion seen through the Loch Rannoch birches — 23

Wade's "masterpiece": the bridge over the River Tay at Aberfeldy — 24

Near Kinloch at the turn-off to Little Glenshee — 25

The Falls of Lochay, visited last century by Charles Dickens — 26

Crossing the ford over the Shochie Burn near Little Glenshee farm — 28

The view north to Meall Buidhe from Stuchd an Lochain, above Glen Lyon — 30

Outstanding bird-watching country: Taymouth Castle woods and Drummond Hill — 34

Peewits' nest near Loch Moraig, Blair Atholl — 36

Whooper swan family group, Loch an Daimh — 38

Cock bullfinch, a none-too-welcome fruit tree visitor — 39

In upper Glen Almond, good territory for cuckoos and ring ouzels — 42

Dipper and sandpiper habitat: the shore of Loch Rannoch — 44

From close beside the Heart Wood: Aberfeldy, Weem Rock and Farragon — 46

Autumn colour show: the track by the Tay near Dunkeld cathedral — 49

Past history: the former poplar avenue between Aberfeldy and Weem — 50

A glimpse of the Hermitage folly through the River Braan woods — 52

An August walk in the Black Wood of Rannoch — 54

One of the old Scots pines near Camghouran — 55

The General Wade portrait on the wall of Weem Inn — 60

The inscription on the parapet of Wade's bridge, Aberfeldy — 61

Typical "Wade": where his road crosses the Lurg Burn near Newton Bridge, Glen Almond — 62

One of the miniature bridges on the Wade road opposite Scotston — 63

Once a problem for Wade's "highwaymen": Clach Ossian in the Sma' Glen — 65

A Highland "woolly bully" encountered while following the old Wade road — 66

A fine 120-ft fall: Black Spout near Pitlochry — 72

The falls of Acharn on the south side of Loch Tay — 74

Moness Falls at the head of the Aberfeldy Birks — 75

One of the falls in the gorge of the River Bruar — 78

Buchanty Spout, well-known salmon leap on the River Almond — 80

Rock architecture in the gorge of the River Bruar — 82

In Glen Tilt: the Bedford memorial bridge — 86

Near the summit of Carn Liath, one of the three Beinn a' Ghlo Munros — 87

On the lochside road near the Black Wood of Rannoch — 88

Loch Tay and the Ben Lawers group from the track above Kenmore — 90

Looking up Loch Katrine from the summit of Ben A'an — 91

Winter walk among the pines above Camghouran — 95

INTRODUCTION

THE measuring of enjoyment — to risk stating the obvious — is not exactly simple. The more one considers it, and certainly the more one tries to write about it, the vaguer its boundaries become. So it is with this small book. To think again of the Perthshire hills and woods, the bird haunts and waterfalls and moorland tracks, is to realise — and not just with personal regrets for all the missed opportunities in days that are past — something of the limitless variety which others with far different tastes can so easily sample and enjoy.

For the young and fit there is little need of any nudging to the imagination; they have a full calendar of good things, from ski-mountaineering in the early months to summer exploits by canoe or rubber dinghy. For the more sedate — or might it be for the lazier? — there could be explorations and wanderings over the less frequented tops away from all Munros and Corbetts; there are the gardens and the castles, the archaeology and the fishing, the alpine plants and the butterfly haunts; always the search for "foods from the woods", from blaeberries and brambles to the fungi-hunting of the experts. The list runs pleasantly on . . . hopefully, in the chapters which follow, helped with an occasional hint.

★ ★ ★

SINCERE thanks go to a number of contributors to enjoyment.

Iain Campbell, kindly helpful with his pick-up truck, must have had many quiet chuckles over the odd ploys of two ageing cyclists. So, too, must the postbus drivers Jim Macdonald and Bob Cassidy, who added rich local commentaries to their very welcome co-operation.

As companions on our woodland walks there could have been none more knowledgeable or more interesting than our good friends and forestry experts Gunnar Godwin, Tavish Macmillan and Jim Chapman. Alan Drever, too, though never out with us in person, provided much enthusiastic and valuable woodlands information.

For photographs, grateful thanks go to George Thomson L.R.P.S., John Wiseman and Mrs Meg Dunn; also to librarian Douglas Spence and *The Courier*, Dundee, for the print of the old Aberfeldy poplar avenue. Details of the Perthshire Mountain Club story, as well as the print showing the club's quaich and aneroid, came from Michael Taylor, deputy curator, Perth Museum and Art Gallery. Helpful Journal excerpts were supplied by Colin Stead, honorary librarian of the Scottish Mountaineering Club, with permission for their use kindly granted by the Editor, Dr Ken Crocket. And throughout the devious paths of production, head librarian James Guthrie, of Perth and Kinross District Libraries, along with Bill Lockhart and Helen Harcus of Sunprint, added to their expertise a welcome bonus of kindliness and patience.

Nearer home, our son Kenneth delved generously into his impressive store of poems to add his own imaginative contributions. And companion on almost every outing, my wife Mais, brought up in a Highland glen and with a deep love of all country things, helped us on in every possible way with unflagging enthusiasm.

To Mais
companion in enjoyment,
with love

ENJOYING WAYS ON THE HILLS

High View

The loch lies like an adder, flecked
With a play of light. Summer orchids blow
On the hill's back, over a turned shoulder
Luminous far sea in dragon scales swims through white.
Here in the high quiet, nothing breathes
Except a mote of eagle in the blue's eye.

MEMORIES of the Perthshire hills go back a long way now. Good memories they are, too, and happily not all blurred beyond recovery by the drifting mists of the years.

There was, for example, the far-off day in the mid-thirties when my brother Colin and I climbed the "anvil peak", Stob Inneoin or, more popularly, Stobinian. Not, in fact, that it was our first visit, only it had its differences. We had travelled by train from Glasgow on the old Oban line as far as the Kingshouse halt and from there set off on foot along the Balquhidder road, bound for the one-time Monachyle youth hostel. It was two days before the New Year and our clinker-nailed boots clattered merrily on the frost-bound road. After a leisurely brew-up at the hostel, we started off for our peak, my diary noting — without any obvious sense of guilt — that by then the time was 12.30 p.m. The weather was anything but encouraging: low mist trailing in long swathes on the far side of the Allt Carnaig corrie; higher, on Stobinian's two subsidiary tops, Meall na Dige and Stob Coire an Lochan, snow falling gently from a sullen cloud-ceiling. Visibility worsened steadily as we climbed; on the bleak backbone of the Stob it was down to a dubious 30 yards. We paused, debating whether or not to carry on to the main top, still some 400 feet above us. The idea of descent was tempting, but as we had toiled upwards thus far, it seemed foolish to call retreat. Fortunately we went on — and had more than adequate reward. Suddenly, just below the summit cairn, we burst through the muggy mist-curtain into a new world, a world of unlimited sunshine and freezing Arctic cold. For the first few moments it was impossible to grasp the change. Apart from the cotton wool carpet at our feet and all around us, not a cloud was to be seen anywhere. Four islands, ragged black skerries, stood clear of the cloud-sea against the ice blue of the sky — our own, Ben More, Beinn Chaluim and Ben Lawers — a quartet of summits we were to come to know well in those early days on the hills. It was the sort of panorama to remember for a lifetime; now, sixty years on, its colours seem as sharp and vivid as on that late afternoon at the tail end of the year.

It is certainly in winter that the Crianlarich hills are at their best, and memory recalls another outstanding — and very different — day on them some years after our Stobinian surprise. It was late February and superlative, set-fair weather, a spell of bitter frost gripping the snow-bound hills iron hard. A start from Inverarnan, in Glen Falloch, well before dawn saw me with the first of the sunshine up at the cairn of Beinn Chabhair with the whole long day stretching ahead. An Caisteal and Beinn a' Chroin followed, sheer delight in each crest and dip and hummock, the hot February sunshine no mean additional bonus. It was not until I reached the corrie-bowl below Beinn Tulaichean that leg-weariness in the sun-softened snow began to take serious toll. The walk had become a trudge and the trudge a treadmill. Even step-counting, that last resort of the enfeebled, was losing its effectiveness. For all of the 1500-ft rise to Beinn Tulaichean it was slow going; for the further 700 feet to its higher neighbour, Cruach Ardrain, fifth Munro of the day, it was airier and so much pleasanter. With that, however, I was slowed to a standstill. Perhaps it was as well: a traverse on my own of Stobinian, and descent of Ben More in the dark, down its long northern slope of frost-hardened snow, might have been less than wholly prudent. In theory it

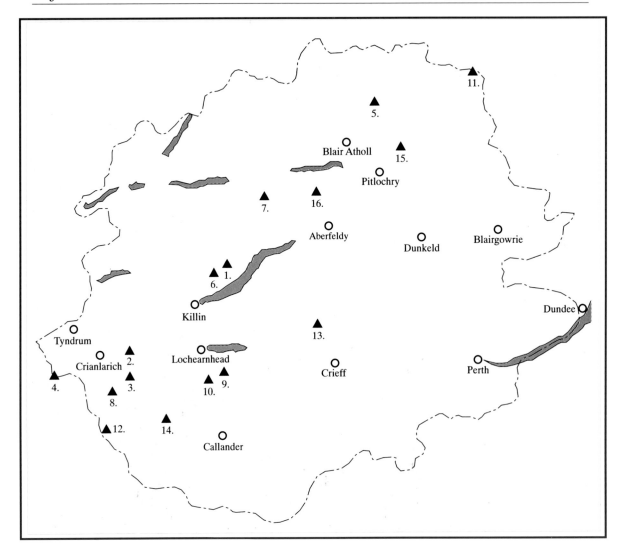

Hills

1.	Ben Lawers,	3984 ft.	9.	Beinn Voirlich,	3224 ft.
2.	Ben More,	3843 ft.	10.	Stuc a'Chroin,	3189 ft.
3.	Stobinian,	3827 ft.	11.	The Cairnwell,	3059 ft.
4.	Beinn Laoigh,	3708 ft.	12.	Beinn Chabhair,	3053 ft.
5.	Beinn a'Ghlo,	3671 ft.	13.	Beinn Chonzie,	3048 ft.
6.	Beinn Ghlas,	3657 ft.	14.	Ben Ledi,	2883 ft.
7.	Schiehallion,	3547 ft.	15.	Ben Vrackie,	2757 ft.
8.	Cruach Ardrain,	3428 ft.	16.	Farragon.	2559 ft.

was disappointing; if truth be told, I was immensely thankful to drop down without further hesitation into the furrow of the Allt Coire Ardrain and so to the fleshpots of Crianlarich.

The north-west face of Cruach Ardrain, grooved by its classic Y Gully, has always held an attraction for winter climbers. An account by Sir Hugh Munro, in a *Scottish Mountaineering Club Journal* of almost a century ago*, typifies the enthusiasm of the early explorers of the Highland hills:

Saturday, 2nd March, was an ideal winter day, clear and bright, with a north-west wind, and not too much of it, though that little was cold; any number of degrees of frost, and everything as dry and hard as bricks. "King Kodak" was responsible for a late start, and it was 10.10 before W. Douglas and H.T. Munro left Crianlarich. Three quarters of an hour later we were in Corrie Ardrain, and in consequence of the hardness of the snow obliged to put on the rope. From here we had two and a half hours' hard cutting up from 700 to 800

feet; the angle was nowhere great, but the snow hard. We made for the saddle between the two tops of Cruach Ardrain, on reaching which it takes only a few minutes to either of the summits, the N.E. of which we topped at 2.30. The height is 3477 feet. From here, discarding the rope, we made our way to Beinn Tulaichean, 3099 feet. Then returning in our steps for some way, we made for the col between Cruach Ardrain and Stob Garbh, from which descending the Ardrain burn we reached the inn in an hour and ten minutes. We had been out exactly eight hours.

Another clear personal memory — again of a climb long past — clamours for mention in the record. It was on a day of late January, noteworthy once more for its biting frost and unbroken, dazzling sunshine. The peak was Beinn Laoigh, dominant on the rampart ranged along Perthshire's south-western border, our objective the mountain's Central Gully, a classic winter route. It was in fact our introduction to genuine snow-climbing and always in later years an

Schiehallion from the east, beyond Loch Kinardochy.

*Scottish Mountaineering Club Journal.
Vol.III. No.17. May 1895.

11

unfailingly popular choice. Out of the sun in the corrie beyond Coninish farm, we entered a sea of cold grey shadow, and I well remember how, all the way up the steepening wall above, our trail of footprints behind us showed black and spidery against the dull surface of the snow. The cornice needed vigorous cutting by the rope leader and we were soon impatiently chilly as we waited and watched in its shadow. Then, in one unforgettable moment, as we poked our heads one by one through the gap, the view suddenly extended from a few grey feet in front of our noses to seemingly limitless miles, miles of a sun-bathed, unbelievably brilliant patchwork of silver peaks and burnt umber moors. Briefly we basked beside the ice-dome of the cairn only yards away, then, from lower on the northern shoulder, dropped back down to less exalted levels in a series of glissades as exhilarating as any I can remember. Beyond the corrie-floor and the farm, on our final homeward tramp down the frost-rutted track to the road, the *Alpenglüh* was tinting the snow-wall of the Crianlarich hills; slowly it faded as radiance took over the pallor of the full January moon.

Beinn Laoigh, or Ben Lui in its anglicised form, is generally accepted to mean "calf peak", and indeed one ought, presumably, to bow before the wisdom of the experts. Yet I have before me a letter addressed to me a number of years ago by a correspondent interested in something I had written about the hill, which puts a different interpretation on the name.

In my boyhood the English spelling was Lui, and I venture to suggest it comes nearer the original *luidhe* meaning "lead". My authority for the suggestion was my own grandmother who lived part of her childhood at Inverarnan in Glen Falloch. I was accustomed to ask her the meaning of Gaelic words and among them was Ardlui. She said it was called Ardlui because lead ore from Ben Lui was brought there in panniers on horses and loaded into gabbarts and taken to Balloch for smelting. The history of lead mining on the Ben goes back, I believe, nearly 250 years. On the other hand, in *Place Names of Dunbartonshire*, John Irving (who incidentally was superintendent of the Sunday school where I had the honour to learn my Catechism) has the meaning of Ardlui as the point where the calves were wont to wade into the water to cool themselves.

My correspondent's suggestion sent me to my Gaelic dictionary, where I found that lead is indeed *luaidh* or *luaidhe*. This further tied in interestingly with the fact that there are two hills named Meall Luaidhe overlooking Glen Lyon, one on the north side a "top" of 3035 feet in the Carn Mairg range, the other, on the south side, a 2558-ft. shoulder of Ben Lawers some seven miles further up the glen. It seems safe enough to say that it would be to the first of these two hills that a paragraph in the Fortingall parish section of the old *Statistical Account* refers:

> There are several small veins of lead ore, jutting out here and there, in the rocks, behind Fortingall. There is one in Glen Lyon, that had been wrought for a short space, about 60 years ago; but it did not answer the expense. Perhaps this was, in some measure, owing to there being no roads in the country at that time (everything being then carried on horseback), which occasioned too much expense, in transporting the ore, etc.

Certainly it is small wonder that the working in Glen Lyon should have had so short a life. It must have been no easy task carrying a cumbersome load of lead ore along the rough, twisting riverside path even as far as Fortingall. By comparison the neighbourhood of Beinn Laoigh would at least have been considerably less remote.

Only that name remained a puzzle. Surely, I decided, Glen Lyon had provided the answer — until the discovery of a reference to "Beinlaoi" in the *Statistical Account* took me right back once again 200 years to where we started, to the familiar confines of square one. "Oh, let us never, never doubt what nobody is sure about!"

The old Beinn Laoigh mines are, in fact, situated on the shoulder of its close neighbour, Meall Odhar, overlooking Tyndrum, and over the years they have had a particularly chequered history. In 1739 they were leased by the Earl of Breadalbane to an Englishman, Sir Robert Clifton, after whom the small village where his workers lived was named. Unfortunately, as he was a supporter of the Jacobite cause, his installations were wrecked by the anti-Jacobite Campbells. Taken over by the Mine Adventurers of England, the mines passed a short time later into the hands of the Scots Mining Company, who built a local smelting works in order to avoid the heavy costs of transporting the ore by road to Loch Lomond and thence to Glasgow. Even this enterprise, however, does not seem to have prospered for long. By the 1790s, according to the Killin parish details, once again in the *Statistical Account*, times were decidedly lean:

> Clifton is a small village, which lies in the west end of the parish. It contains about 200 persons, who have hitherto earned their bread principally in working in a lead mine. ...... This has been wrought for these 40 years past, but it is given up for the present, which proves a temporary inconvenience to the poor people in its neighbourhood, who depended chiefly for their subsistence upon the employment they got in it.

The old tracks and galleries may, of course, still be seen today, sad grey scars on the hillside above Tyndrum, and for anyone so minded, it is possible to explore the shafts — with care.

Delving into the diary to recapture the essence of days that are past can provide fireside fun in plenty. Yet what a vast amount goes wholly un-remembered! How often one has to take oneself to task for the abysmal laziness that has left an endless string of details never recorded! In the early days of novelty, of course, there was every reason to wax garrulous and syrupy with descriptions; less excuse more recently for brevity, usually an admission of crude slavishness to time, a slavishness which might even go so far as to produce an entry: "23.9.72: Meall a' Choire Leith (3033 ft.) ↑1 hour 35 minutes; ↓ 48 minutes."

Probably it is the weather which makes for most variety in the diary entries, whether they be long or short. A storm force wind in July 1987 had my wife and me almost scree-scrabbling on hands and knees in such shelter as we could find to reach the summit cairn of Beinn Ghlas; on a September day 55 years before, the gale, I see, was no less ferocious. Fog-crystals were dangling like stalactites from that same cairn, and the far hump of Ben Nevis was out-

Ben More and Stobinian from near Crianlarich

standing in the view, ghostly white with the first snowfalls of winter.

A war-time memory dates back to New Year's Day 1943 and weather as disagreeable as one could ever wish for on the hill. Again it was the old Oban line which proved an invaluable help, taking my companion, the late Norman Easton, and me on an early train from Glasgow to Strathyre. The hill of our choice was Stuc a' Chroin (3189 feet), near neighbour to Ben Voirlich, our (pre-blanket afforestation days) approach up and over the whaleback ridge behind the village. The first slope was a harsh treadmill in shin-deep new snow and we were thankful to reach the high hummocks between Beinn Each and the Stuc itself. Not indeed that there was any real respite on this last lap to the top, as the biting north-easter kept flinging squall after squall of snow in our faces all the way to the cairn. We certainly needed no urging to hurry on the three-mile return down the glen to Loch Lubnaig, where the gale was still tossing spindrift from the wicked grey turmoil of wave-crests.

There was in fact an amusing irony in this Arctic scenario, as Norman was briefly on leave from No.5 Commando, just back from a duty-stint in the tropical oven heat of Madagascar. We were to recall the day often enough too, later in the year, when training in Mediterranean balminess on the granite sea-cliffs of Cornwall.

Unpredictable rather than merely churlish is no doubt the fairest description of the weather on the tops. One contrast comes readily to mind — between days this time on Crieff's familiar "back-door" Munro, Ben Chonzie. An ascent towards the end of December with my daughter Helen not so very many years ago was sugges-tive of a crossing of the polar ice-cap. The sum-mit plateau carried a heavy deposit of snow, hard frozen, and the shrill half-gale out of the north stung and harried us mercilessly, whip-ping up clouds of ice-spicules like spindrift against our faces. The big untidy cairn had the look of a tumbledown igloo, and there was little comfort in its shelter, so that we were not sorry to turn tail, scurry down — skis, or even a nice

Lochan nan Cat and An Stuc, a subsidiary "top" of Ben Lawers.

roomy sledge would have been welcome — and thaw out again at lower levels. By contrast, on another occasion right on the brink of winter, when I was again on Ben Chonzie with my daughter, the weather was so kindly that she opted for a pause to have a bathe. I for my part, being of altogether sterner stuff, was able to resist the temptation.

One particularly enterprising visitor to the hills of Perthshire back at the start of the nineteenth century was Dr John Macculloch, army surgeon, mineralogist and indefatigable traveller. His four-volume book, *The Highlands and Western Isles of Scotland*, makes thoroughly rewarding and often highly humorous reading despite the fact that in parts it is long-winded and boastful almost beyond endurance. For example, Macculloch claims with typical lack of modesty, "I have ascended almost every principal mountain in Scotland." Yet his list of ascents is in fact impressive enough for those early days — a dozen Munros and as many lesser hills — while his other exploits, from Ailsa Craig to St Kilda, the Flannans and North Rona, from Cluny's Cage on Ben Alder and a crossing of Rannoch Moor to negotiation of Corryvreckan in his ship's longboat, are certainly not lacking in interest. Four of the Munros which he bagged were in Perthshire — Ben Lawers, Beinn a' Ghlo, Schiehallion and

Ben Chonzie — and to these he added the lesser tops of Ben Ledi and Ben Venue. Not surprisingly in the course of his travels he met with some really wild weather. It had snowed hard on the summit plateau of Ben Nevis, although for the ultimate in discomfort it was Ben Ledi that he singled out: "I thought that I had known Highland rain in all its forms and mixtures and varieties; but nothing like the rain on Ben Ledi did I ever behold, before or since."

Like many another hill-walker since his day, Macculloch chose Ben Lawers as the most outstanding mountain viewpoint in Scotland. As he comments,

Ben Lomond alone can compete with it for the view from the summit; but there is a much greater variety of country seen from this hill, and the range is also greater. It is also a great advantage in this case, that Ben Lawers towers over all the hills immediately near it, by more than a thousand feet, and that it has no competitor in altitude nearer than Ben More, which, while it is also inferior, is so remote as not to obstruct the view. It is impossible to describe the variety and splendour of this, the most magnificent of our mountain views.

It is not surprising that Ben Lawers was an important centre in the network of the Great Triangulation of the United Kingdom in 1852. It was linked by direct sights to stations in Jura

Snow-patches and sunshine at the top of Ben Vrackie.

(80 miles distant), Ben Nevis, Ben Macdhui, Ben More in Mull, The Merrick in Galloway and other peaks — components of an impressive panorama indeed. Probably the finest view of Ben Lawers itself is from the east, preferably from high on the hillside above Kenmore, with half of Loch Tay a foreground of endlessly changing moods and patterns. Snow-covered, brilliant in morning sunshine, bisected by the long scimitar sweep of the east ridge, this face of the mountain has all the magnificence of a peak in the Bernese Oberland.

In Dr Macculloch's day the accepted height of Ben Lawers was 4015 feet, probably as calculated back in 1774 by that remarkable mapmaker, William Roy. In the Kenmore parish report in the *Statistical Account* it is given passing mention:

> Of these mountains, Ben Lawers is by far the highest, being 4015 feet above the level of the sea, and is said to be the second highest mountain in Scotland. While I write this, being the 16th of May, 1795, it is covered with new laid snow, a considerable way down its sides. It abounds with many rare plants, and is frequented by a great variety of quadrupeds and fowls.

As a result of the Great Triangulation Ben Lawers was demoted from its august place in the ranks of the fourthousanders to a mere 3984 feet, a drop from "second" place to ninth among Scottish heights. This caused so much annoyance to one lover of Perthshire, Mr Malcolm Ferguson, a native of Morenish near Killin and devoted to the country of Breadalbane, that he decided action must be taken to rectify the situation. It is often recalled how, on 4th July 1878, he and a party of some 30 local volunteers erected a massive cairn at the summit to bring the mountain once more above the exalted 4000-ft level, toil for which each of his helpers was generously rewarded with a "handsome volume of Gaelic poetry." Hopes were no doubt high that this masterpiece of construction engineering would be long-lasting, but weather and tourists played swift havoc, and in remarkably few years very little was to be seen of the old cairn.

Sadly it has to be admitted that the splendid opportunities for skiing offered by the grassy hills of the Lawers group have largely passed me by. True, we have had our quota of winter sorties from the car-park at the National Trust for Scotland visitor centre. But these have been family affairs spent for the most part in chilly discomfort trying to get the better of the children's unco-operative skis. This is not a pastime to be recommended. Skies may be cloudless blue, the sun shining free, but old-fashioned bindings repeatedly coming adrift and iron-stiff with frozen snow can be guaranteed to play havoc with almost any day's enjoyment.

Yet if personal experiences have been somewhat mixed, at least imagination is left free to picture some of the sport that has been enjoyed by enthusiasts hereabouts over the years. It was in 1907 that the Scottish Ski Club was formed, and for half a century, before mechanisation on Meall a' Bhuiridh first highlighted the rival attractions of Glencoe, Ben Lawers and its satellites provided a real Mecca for the faithful. Rain, hail or shine, they came to know and appreciate the delights of the easy running in the gentle-angled bowl of Coire Odhar (where at 2500 feet the club hut was erected in 1932), of more testing traverses high on the ridges of Beinn Ghlas and Meall Corranaich, and often enough of further exploration far beyond.

The lively interest these days in cross-country ski-ing and ski-mountaineering is apt to suggest that such variations are something of a novelty. True, for many they are an increasingly popular breakaway from the more conventional piste running of the "downhill only" thousands. Yet even a brief look at the enterprise of the early enthusiasts makes clear how exploration of the high tops and corries, far beyond the confines of the Lawers playground, had its devotees from the first.

Back in 1891 W.W. Naismith, "father" of the Scottish Mountaineering Club, describes exhilarating running on the Campsie Fells, and incidentally finds it necessary to give details of his skis — "wooden snow-skates, 7 feet long and 3 to 4 inches wide, largely used throughout the northern parts of Europe and Asia." In 1905 we read of another early president of the Scottish Mountaineering Club, Harry MacRobert, being introduced to the sport on the Pentlands and ending the day at midnight by skiing down the tramlines to Morningside station in Edinburgh.

In March of the previous year another enthusiast, J.H. Wigner, one of the leading spirits in the formation of the Scottish Ski Club, had had a memorable Perthshire day climbing Ben Chonzie on ski. Taking an early train to Crieff, he was clear of the "village" by 10 a.m., surprised and delighted that "the sight of a pair of ski did not gather a mob." From Loch Turret he climbed to the subsidiary top of Carn Chois (2571 feet) and from the col beyond to the plateau of Ben Chonzie itself. His actual ski-running does not appear to have been particularly noteworthy, but the comments he makes on his day are interesting for their assessment of worth-while future opportunities:

> The snow throughout the day was in ideal condition, and the hills, although quite uninteresting from the climber's point of view, are perfect for ski-running. Ben Chonzie being very broad and flat-topped has a large area above the 2,000 contour, and being situated in a district of pretty heavy rainfall, usually carries a good deal of snow till quite late in the season. A pleasant variation of this trip would be a traverse from Crieff to Comrie, or *vice versa*, or the complete circuit of the hills around Loch Turret.*

Still taking a backward glance at the old days, it is easily seen what rich variety would be available to members of the Perthshire Mountain Club, a highly intriguing subsidiary of the Perthshire Society of Natural Science. This remarkable offshoot club was started in 1875 — that is, no less than 14 years before the founding of the Cairngorm Club and Scottish Mountaineering Club, the two clubs usually given pride of place in Scottish mountaineering history. Details are tantalisingly scanty, but now and again — especially in the *Transactions and Proceedings* of the parent society — the mists are parted slightly to allow some fascinating glimpses of great days long past.

There was nothing half-hearted about the way the club was run. For example, only those members of the Society who had climbed a Perthshire mountain of at least 3000 feet were eligible for election, their initiation taking place at the summit cairns where official meets were customarily held. Office-bearers numbered five. Of these the Cairnmaster, or president, and the Scribe and Annalist, or secretary, need no explanation. The Quaich-bearer, fairly obviously, had charge of the club's small silver

quaich, which had its part in the initiation rites, doubtless with suitably generous helpings of mountain dew. The Geometer was charged with the weighty responsibility of making sure that members had reached the necessary altitude, a task for which he was provided with a pocket aneroid barometer. Finally there was the Bard, whose duty was the most arduous of all — the

At the top of Central Gully near the summit of Beinn Laoigh.

composition of a special poem for each mountain meet, a work which does not seem to have been restricted to a mere two or three verses, as is apparent in some of the effusions preserved in the club records. Interestingly, too, both aneroid and quaich are still kept at Perth Museum and Art Gallery. The former is inscribed "P.S.N.S. (Mountain Club) Perth", the latter with "Perthshire Mountain Club" and "Salix herbacea floreat", the official dwarf alpine willow motto, inscribed round its rim.

Wretched weather was obviously no excuse for poor performance on the hill. According to a retrospective note in the *Transactions* of 1949: "In the earlier days it was customary for the members of the Mountain Club to be summoned to meet on a certain peak at a certain hour, for

---

in a report of a meeting on Stuc a' Chroin, one of the peaks of Ben Voirlich, it is recorded that the meeting was held in mist and driving rain at the exact hour for which summonses were issued." On another occasion, too, on 4th July 1915, the official record states: "The top of Ben Lawers was reached in the teeth of a violent wind. Sheltered behind the cairn, however, we held the usual meeting of the Mountain Club, and initiated several new members." One can well imagine that on such occasions there was no great doubt as to the popularity of the Quaich-bearer. It went without saying, of course, that the actual summit had to be in Perthshire; thus one walk which started in

The quaich and aneroid which belonged to the Perthshire Mountain Club.
(Perth Museum and Art Gallery.)

Inverness-shire, at Dalwhinnie, could not be recognised as an official meet until the county boundary had been crossed and a "home" peak reached. On the occasion of an ascent of Ben Chonzie, above Crieff, in June 1884, Perth was left at 7.30 a.m. and not reached again on the return until almost midnight. Certainly there can be little doubt about the club's enthusiasm, and although details are hard to come by, it seems — perhaps not surprisingly — to have remained in existence for the best part of 50 years.

From the back door steps of our house in Aberfeldy one can see on clear days the summit tips of three fine hills — Schiehallion (3547 feet), Farragon (2559 feet) and Ben Vrackie (2757 feet). Often in winter they stand out startlingly white with new snow; always, winter or summer, they clamour for visits. Sometimes, in more fanciful moods, it has seemed to me that

climbing these three hills would present a superb one-day challenge. One might, for instance, bivouac high on Ben Vrackie some balmy night in June, pay a quick visit to the summit, then spend the rest of the long day ahead bagging the other two peaks. It might well be a memorable round, if sadly now — even with Himalayan high camp tactics, skilful transport help and obliging family or friends acting as Sherpas — one to be left to the fleeter of foot.

Schiehallion, of course, is a hill to be climbed not just once but many times; indeed a family of our acquaintance find its magnetism so strong that they make a pilgrimage to the top at least once a year. Deep, dark furrows have been worn in its peaty slopes above the car-park near Braes of Foss and these bear witness in no uncertain way to its popularity; nowadays, rain, hail or shine, there can be more than a hint of high street congestion up to and along the mountain's airy quartzite spine.

Schiehallion is another mountain name which seems to present a puzzle to the experts. The late Seton Gordon preferred this spelling to the occasional Schichallion, commenting that in Gaelic it is Sidh Chailleann, meaning "fairy hill of the Caledonians". Presumably this spelling and interpretation had the approval of his friend and frequent adviser, Professor W.J. Watson, the distinguished authority on Celtic place-names. I have, however, seen the meaning given as "nest or brooding place of storms", while the writer of *The Scottish Tourist*, published in 1825, has a different interpretation again, referring to the "enormous Schihallien, insulated from the surrounding mountains, and towering to a height of 3550 feet. This mountain is the reputed haunt of the monstrous fairy Cailin," a suggestion which ties in with the legend that a malignant witch is said to have scarred the face of the hill with her broomstick. Even that is not all, for according to the *Statistical Account* still 30 years before, "Thichallin (which signifies the

Maiden's breast, its form being quite round) is one of the highest hills in the island," while a modern place-name glossary says it is "probably Shin-Chailin — maiden pap."

Our own visits to the hill have hardly matched up to our friends' record of once a year, yet they have had in them a real wealth of enjoyment. The first (so my diary tells me) provided an afternoon romp up and down of 2¼ hours; now our most recent visit, a family affair half a century later, took slightly more than twice as long — a day in mid-November when a storm-force gale, whining and thundering murderously round the summit blocks, had us all but admitting eleventh hour defeat. We were late — no doubt reprehensibly late — on the hill that afternoon and it was well after dark before we were back at the car at Braes of Foss.

Although almost 200 feet higher than Farragon, our nearest neighbour — 2757 feet as against 2559 feet — Ben Vrackie has a way of seeming a much easier, kindlier hill to climb. On the usual approach-march to Farragon, even the fact that one can take the car up some 700 feet to above Glassie farm makes surprisingly little difference to the tedium. On the other hand, Ben Vrackie, with its pleasant start through the Moulin woods and further on little Loch a' Choire set picturesquely at the foot of the final pyramid, has a variety that is much more satisfying.

Of three fairly recent visits to Ben Vrackie it is difficult to decide which was the most enjoyable: in spring across the heather from a point high above Pitlochry on the Kirkmichael road, when the curlews and larks and meadow pipits were at their musical best; in autumn when the trees above Moulin seemed almost to be on fire with colour, or on a day of summer so gloriously warm that the female members of other parties on the hill were climbing in déshabille more suited to Mediterranean beaches than to the sober slopes of the Central Highlands. My only regret is that I cannot complete a quartet of seasonal comparisons by telling of a winter visit on ski.

Near neighbour of Ben Vrackie, Beinn a' Ghlo the "mountain of mist" has a much more complex make-up of ridge and corrie. It has, in fact, four summits, of which three are regarded as separate Munros, while it is said that in any one of its nineteen corries a rifle can be fired with-out being heard in any other. The usual approach is over Carn Liath (3193 feet) from a starting-point near little Loch Moraig, and the comments in my diary are not really necessary for me to recall vividly the scorching heat of one visit which we paid in early May when the turf and screes seemed to climb ahead of us for ever. So Saharan indeed was the heat, so interminable the upward plod, that I began to have a real fellow-feeling for Shakespeare's Falstaff who, according to Prince Henry

..... sweats to death,
And lards the lean earth as he walks along.

Once on the first summit, however, the battle has been largely won and if time allows there is a superb high-level walk beyond over the other three tops, with far views on every side.

In her Highland *Journal* Queen Victoria, when staying at Blair Castle, is generous in her praise of Beinn a' Ghlo and Glen Tilt. The first of her half dozen Munros was Carn a' Chlamain, on the opposite side of Glen Tilt to Beinn a' Ghlo. The September day, the Queen noted, "was glorious and it would have been a pity to lose it, but it was a long hard day's work, though extremely delightful and enjoyable, and unlike anything I had ever done before." At the summit "the view was quite beautiful, nothing but mountains all around us, and the solitude, the complete solitude, very impressive." Progress, however, was slow, as Albert was trying, unsuccessfully, for a stag, so that on the way down they did not regain the floor of the glen until after dark. "We walked to the Marble Lodge, and then got into the pony carriage and drove home by very bright moonlight, which made everything look very lovely; but the road made one a little nervous." The Queen at that time was only 25 years old, but she had to wait for another four years before there was an opportunity for further peak-bagging. On Lochnagar and Ben Macdhui she was much less fortunate with the weather, although on Beinn a' Bhuird visibility was good and on the rolling moorland tops above the Cairnwell pass the sun was to shine for her just as lavishly as it had done on that first outing to Carn a' Chlamain. The Queen's descriptions of all these expeditions — long, exacting days mostly on pony-back and more than once in wind, rain and biting cold — add up to a remarkable portrait of her far different from that so commonly and so unfairly held.

19

To give any more than passing mention to that group of hills round the Cairnwell pass on the borders of Perthshire, Aberdeenshire and Angus might be thought to savour more than a little of anti-climax. By no stretch of the imagination are they at all dramatic: their slopes are gentle, their summit plateaux broad and rounded. Indeed, in the course of innumerable visits, it might perhaps be fair to say that the occasion of greatest peril was one evening on Carn a' Gheoidh during the rutting season, when a stag emerged belligerently from dense mist to look me up and down and decide, fortunately, that I wasn't worthy of battle. Yet to disregard these hills completely would undoubtedly be wrong. Over the years they have given so much enjoyment that to write them off as insignificant would be ungrateful indeed.

Perhaps some of the interest has evaporated with the elimination of the old Devil's Elbow. There was something of challenge in driving alone over the pass at one o'clock of a January morning with a film of ice on the road, or running back once the worst of the climb was over to help push a fellow-traveller whose car-wheels were spinning despairingly. Things are different now, with the road straightened, gradients eased and care taken to ensure that the thousands of visiting skiers are not trapped at the top of the pass by the fiercest of the winter blizzards.

Strictly speaking, none of these Munros is wholly in Perthshire. Creag Leacach (3238 feet) stands on the Angus border, while Carn a' Gheoidh (3194 feet) and The Cairnwell (3059 feet) are half in Aberdeenshire. "Cairnwell" is the anglicised version of a name that is centuries old. As far back as the year 1630 the Carnavalage or Carnavalay was listed as one of eleven routes over the mountains from the River Tay to the River Dee. Many of the hills round about have "Carn" as the first part of their names, and one above Gleann Beag, running down to the Spittal of Glenshee — Carn aig Mhala, (pronounced Carn ag Vala, and meaning "cairn at the brow of the hill") — seems to be quite a reasonable clue to the explanation of "Cairnwell".

With the highest point of the pass 2199 feet, it can be seen that a visit to the top of The Cairnwell itself, only 860 feet above, is not particularly exacting; indeed, I find from my diary that up and down one December day of new snow needed just 38 minutes — and that time could surely be much bettered without any difficulty at all. Nowadays mention of Glenshee and the hills above the old Elbow is apt to conjure up pictures of chairlifts and ski-tows straggling untidily to the bounding skylines. To some the mechanisation and accompanying scars are offensive and sad; to others they are essentially the pointers to exhilarating, high-speed winter adventure. Fortunately the day has not yet arrived — and may it still remain a while round a distant corner — when a chairborne approach to the top of The Cairnwell might even be a welcome means of ascent, a humble way of recapturing just a fraction of the joys of days that are past on so many of the Perthshire tops.

Schiehallion

The hill is a pyramid
Lifted by arid slaves
Sometime when restless volcanoes
Dragoned and hissed these lands.

The hill is an arrowhead
Shaped out of bare flint
Set against the cave darkness
Of flames, a hunter's sunset.

The hill is a jagged finger
Still raised in ancient accusation
Towards God's midges — men
Who dare to climb her spine.

ENJOYING CYCLING DOWN THE MAP

Song: *The Empty Glens*

I heard a man crying away on a hillside
The wind in his plaid and his staff lifted high
Where now the wild orchids we gathered in summer
And who hears the songs of the men of the glens?

The well-mouth is covered where tall grow the rushes
The peat fire is cold and the plough rusty lies
No children to glean from the hoard of the squirrel
And none hears the songs of the men of the glens.

Our homes they have burned, and our people have scattered
To cross the wide seas, or to toil in the towns
Our lands they have taken for sheep and their shepherds
And have silenced the songs of the men of the glens.

The rowans in autumn still bear their red clusters
The sandpiper's note is still heard by the burn
The curlews still cry over lonely Strathnaver
But gone are the songs of the men of the glens.

THE WILDLY tossing trees and the tall grasses along the roadside, bent almost horizontal by the sheer frenzy of the gale, spoke only too eloquently of the shape of things to come. Thinking of the two bicycles lying behind us on the floor of the pick-up truck, I averted my gaze from the wind-whipped verges and tried my hardest to concentrate on the road ahead.

My wife and I were bound for Dalnaspidal. Our intention: to cycle from there across country to Loch Rannoch and Kinloch Rannoch, the first leg of a hill-track ride north-south down Perthshire. Initially we had succumbed to a temptation which had been dangling in front of us for years — to follow the old drove road south along the shore of Loch Garry, set so alluringly in the depression between its low, flanking hills, and seen beckoning every time we passed up or down the A9. Looked at on the map, the venture seemed both practicable and attractive: a track of double dots for 3½ miles to the far end of Loch Garry and another double-dotted continuation from a point a mile farther on. The gap in between looked to be easily bridged by a spider-web link of single dots — and the eye of faith. We were full of confidence. What our good friend Iain Campbell was thinking as he drove the pick-up through the tugging, tearing cross-wind, we had no idea. He was much too polite to tell us.

We stopped at Dalnaspidal Lodge to make enquiries, watching as we waited for the response to our knock, how a flock of recently arrived fieldfares was being tossed off course by the gale like a flurry of autumn leaves. Yes, we were told, it would probably be possible to cycle through to Loch Rannoch. No, there would be no objection so far as the stalking was concerned this side of the march; and as there was no reply to a phoned enquiry, it would probably be all right on the far side also. We said goodbye to Iain. Hopefully we would meet again at Kinloch Rannoch in the afternoon. He gave us kindly looks and words of encouragement, no doubt wondering if we had our survival kits with us. The wind was buffeting us as viciously as ever. Ruefully I recalled that it was the equinox.

A momentary hint of optimism that the wind

CYCLING DOWN THE MAP

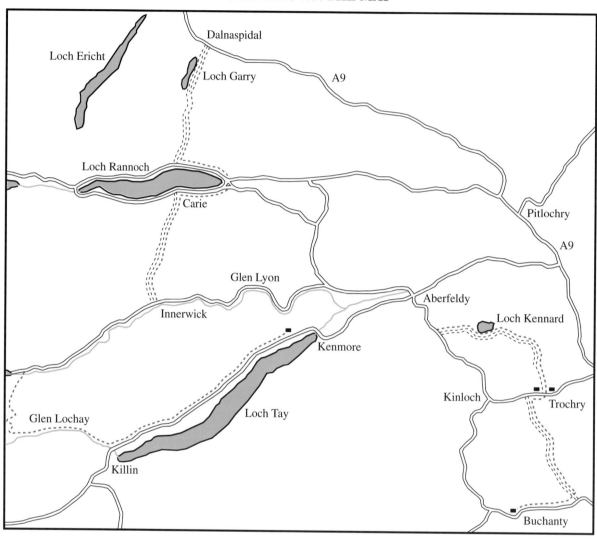

was coming over Drumochter and would in fact be partially behind us, died almost as soon as it was born. The first dozen yards in the saddle brought it brutally home to us: we were to be on a head-on collision course with not the slightest hope of escape. There was nothing we could do but pedal on — whenever the battering allowed us. We kept mounting and re-mounting, unable to keep going for long even on the level. Simply battering our way across the two bridges, over the Allt Dubhaig and the Allt Coire Luidhearnaidh, to the nearer end of the loch took an interminable time. Kinloch Rannoch seemed a very long way off. We wondered if life would have been any kinder had we moved with the times and hired mountain bikes, aggressively geared, instead of trusting to our mounts of simpler, less sophisticated days.

Alongside the loch things were no better. Any hopes that the tilt of the moors would give some shelter were dashed. Indeed the scoop of the loch seemed to act maliciously like a funnel to fling the gale still more fiercely at us in gust after gust. As Mais recalled afterwards, "It was a case of getting on to our bikes when the wind wasn't looking." With every ten yards gained we agreed more and more heartily that the best place to be was somewhere else. Or as Mr Weller senior sagely observed to his son: "I know'd what 'ud come o' this here mode o' doing bisness. Oh Sammy, Sammy, vy worn't there a alleybi!"

In precisely an hour we had reached the mouth of the North of Scotland Hydro-Electric Board's tunnel, a conspicuous white building by the loch-side which had beckoned to us light-

A familiar view of Schiehallion seen through the Loch Rannoch birches.

house-like for all of the 2½ miles we had struggled over, and into whose shelter we flopped like a couple of spent fish. The tunnel was, in fact, built by the Grampian Electricity Supply Company between March 1936 and June 1937, taking water from Loch Garry through to Loch Ericht, five miles distant and at a level lower by 180 feet. Loch Ericht in turn, dammed at its south-western end, is the main storage reservoir for the power station on the shore of Loch Rannoch and has a key role in the Hydro Board's Tummel-Garry scheme. It was amusing to reflect that a drop of water in the loch near where we were sitting might well be about to travel to Kinloch Rannoch, the same destination as ourselves, if by a slower and somewhat more devious route.

But our thoughts during our rest centred rather on more immediate matters, such as making this our first sitting for lunch and wondering if the rest of the trip would be as exacting as the introduction had been. The peace and quiet of our sanctuary certainly made it difficult to appreciate the full fury of the gale. Only the sullen, battleship grey of the loch, white-plumed and angry, reminded us that the fight was most assuredly still on. Perhaps our reluctance to

emerge from shelter and continue was excusable. Yet in the event it was less trying than we had expected. The track, much rougher with ruts and boulders than before, climbed in a series of switchbacks for some threequarters of a mile, so that there was good reason for walking and pushing much of the way. Then, quite emphatically, it came to an end. Ahead lay a desert of wet peat, sphagnum moss and a maze of ditches.

We found it difficult to accept the fact that we had been contemplating the next section through rose-coloured spectacles, that the map's thread of dots smacked of wishful thinking. Perhaps it was as well that we hadn't known before. Now we realised that there was nothing for it but to press on regardless.

In fact, we soon discovered that there was remarkably little difficulty. We had to do battle for the most part with moor-grass on ground that was relatively level, rather than with tough, tussocky heather. Admittedly Loch Garry seemed to take an inordinately long time to drop behind, but nevertheless our progress over the trackless mile was much better than we deserved. It ended on the bank of a river, the Allt Shallainn — a sizeable obstacle. A ford is

Wade's "masterpiece": the bridge over the River Tay at Aberfeldy.

marked on the map, but we failed to find it; instead, quite simply, the bicycles had to be bumped from stone to stone and hoisted up the farther bank. Had the burn been in spate and not especially low after the preceding dry weather, we should have been in trouble indeed.

Beyond the river things looked up. We came to a large sheep-fank and — wonder of wonders — a path of sorts leading through invading moor-grass to the deserted buildings of Duinish. From here on, we knew, there would be no more obstacles, and we relaxed on a mossy bank for second sitting of lunch. The wind was still boisterous, but it had less vindictiveness in it and we were more concerned to see rain clouds moving in. Fortunately the threat was more imaginary than real and although the afternoon did turn misty and damp, it was never unpleasantly wet.

We now had to face a gradual uphill trundle of some 200 feet, but we were confident that our pushing and puffing would be richly rewarded thereafter by the unbroken four-mile descent to Loch Rannoch-side. Rewarded it certainly was, but not as richly as we had expected. Had the surface of the track been really good, the run would have been one of the finest in Perthshire. As it was, we had a hard fight of it all the way. In places the going was sandy and soft, interrupting our headlong career with sudden, unexpected checks; between, the disarray of loose stones set front wheels and handlebars juddering like a horrific succession of pneumatic drills — a particularly disagreeable variation for Mais, as she was still feeling the effects of a recently cracked elbow. The wind, too, seemed to be taking renewed delight in pestering us, and more than once we had to pocket our pride, dismount and walk. However, at least it was all downhill and immensely enjoyable despite the drawbacks. Some day, maybe, we shall do it all again, when the curlews are calling and larks are high overhead, or else at the tail-end of summer with more excuses for halts on the look-out for patches of white heather.

Entering the shelter of a birch wood alongside the Allt a' Chreagain Odhair, the track seemed finally to have given up its stop-go pranks with sandy strips and boulders. The going suddenly was easier, and we made quick time past Craiganour Lodge down to the junction with the main road. Here a glance over our shoulders to a prominent notice informed us that trying con-

Near Kinloch at the turn-off to Little Glenshee.

clusions with the bullets of a high velocity rifle might well be ill-advised.

Thereafter, the final three miles to Kinloch Rannoch were undiluted pleasure. The wind was now well and truly behind us and — almost to our surprise — there was no longer any need to engage in a perilous slalom between rocks small and large. We sailed along at a merry speed past a changing patchwork of early autumn colours, copper of bracken, gold of birch, against the grey of the loch and the mist-topped hills beyond. As we neared Kinloch Rannoch, the blandishments of a notice directing us to a Time-Share beauty salon were not difficult to resist, although we did feel not a little unkempt and wind-blown when eventually we sat down to hotel afternoon tea — or was it third sitting for lunch? Whichever it was, the chicken sandwiches were good, too good indeed to last till Iain Campbell and the pick-up truck arrived to carry us home to Aberfeldy.

★   ★   ★

"ARE YOU away your holidays?" The question thrown at us by one of our neighbours was not really surprising. Brows furrowed to a sizeable interrogation-mark, he was watching us and our cycles — decorated with bundled sleeping-bags and straggling string like so much untidy knitting — departing self-consciously downhill to the main road. The fact that it was almost mid-November and a damp, dreary, misty afternoon into the bargain lent some point to our friend's incredulity. Nor had we time to pause and explain: twenty miles of road from Aberfeldy to Kinloch Rannoch lay ahead of us and we were only too well aware that dark would be setting in early.

No easy option for Mais and me this time; no Iain Campbell with pick-up truck to take us in luxury to the starting-point for the second leg of our southward journey. Instead, we faced three hours and more of hard toil.

In fact the toil went surprisingly well: encouragement as we beat our schedule to Coshieville; the gain only fractionally lost on the long plod up beside the Keltney Burn gorge. Then the Glengoulandie deer farm, where a relaxing "royal" watched us with majestic nonchalance as we trundled past. A pair of whooper swans, starkly white in the gloaming, barked at us from Loch Kinardochy; then down we swooped to the Braes of Foss car-park below Schiehallion, nonexistent in a complete grey-out of mist. Switchbacks took us to Loch an Daimh with its fringe of "lion grass" and tall, matching reeds. Then down again to a breather at East Tempar, with an owl screeching and dozens of greylags chorusing in the growing darkness over towards Dunalastair. At Kinloch Rannoch there was real satisfaction in seeing the signpost "Aberfeldy 20 miles", but hardly as much in that as in the warm fireside welcome from our friend Pat Mitchell, headmistress of the local primary school, with whom we were to enjoy the luxury of an overnight stay.

The plan this time — sequel to our initial run

The Falls of Lochay, visited last century by Charles Dickens.

over the hill from Dalnaspidal — was to cycle the three miles along the south side of Loch Rannoch as far as the cottage cluster at Carie and there part company with the "real" road. The public forestry footpath, climbing for 800 feet and the best part of another four miles, would then take us to the open moorland sloping up to the narrows of the Lairig Chalbhath. Thence we would drop down more abruptly to Innerwick, in Glen Lyon, a further four miles from the forest edge. At 2.10 p.m. the Glen Lyon postbus would pick us up, cycles and all, and carry us in triumph back home to Aberfeldy. In short, we were in total agreement with Mr Weller's profound observation, "The adwantage o' the plan's hobvious."

The following morning was misty, windless and mild — a complete and agreeable contrast to the equinoctial ferocity with which we had been battered at the start of our Dalnaspidal-Kinloch Rannoch outing. Even so it was anything but easy to tear ourselves away from the home comforts which Pat had provided for us and which made all the difference to our enjoyment. A sumptuous breakfast set the seal to her kindness and indeed presented such a strong temptation to laziness that I even had the unworthy idea that we might consider honour to have been satisfied by the toil of the previous evening. Fortunately, however, I was shamed into action, and by 9.30 we were wheeling out our cycles ready for the day ahead.

Nothing, evidently, had damped Mais's enthusiasm. As she pedalled happily away, I sensed that she was on the verge of bursting into song. My own mood was less jocund. I found an aversion to sitting on my saddle that was strangely commanding; it was not difficult to imagine what a morning would be like after taking part in the Calgary Stampede. As we crossed the hump-backed bridge over the Tummel, I looked sourly at an unoffending heron down by the river's edge; he remained unmoving and unmoved.

Fortunately things looked up as we warmed to the morning's work. On the one hand the road-fringe under the birches was patterned gold; on the other, Loch Rannoch, silver smooth, stretched westwards to a misty infinity. There was no breeze, only the autumn scents which somehow seemed to emphasise the stillness. We passed several lochside corners which reminded us of summer picnics of the past. At some, no doubt, there would have been sandpiper pairs keening their anxiety; now they were all deserted and silent, except when once a solitary dipper went whirring away in low gear, inches above the rock-scatterings of the shore.

Forty minutes took us to Carie, where we surprised a trio of jays and put up a gaggle of 18 greylag geese, noisily resentful at having to leave their field and morning feeding. Opposite us, on the far side of the loch, were the cottages of Aulich and Craiganour Lodge, where we had turned to that pleasant last lap of our run over from Dalnaspidal. This time it was a beginning, not an ending: a signpost telling us that it was seven miles by way of the footpath over the hill to Glen Lyon. We wondered how many more miles it would seem to have been by the time the crossing was behind us and we were safely across at Innerwick.

The first part of our climb was sombre and uninspiring, rather too suggestive of the kind of conifer tunnel we are going to have to live with so often in the future. Fortunately the gradient was gradual and we could ride for much of the way, but the world on either hand was one of dark recesses, damp with mosses and lichens. However, there was light at the end of the tunnel — a delightful stretch with an outlook leftwards over the deep den of the burn. Here we bumped over the gnarled roots of pine trees, more characteristic, to my way of thinking, of the true Black Wood of Rannoch than the denser jungle we had left behind. We were on a sandy switchback of short ups and downs, making us question whether it was easier to ride or to walk. Then came a deep, exhilarating swoop, followed by a corresponding toilsome ascent and, further on, an idyllic-looking picnic spot in a clearing, with rustic table set beside a deep, peaty trout pool.

From here to the march fence was a long, long climb, bend after tedious bend through comparatively recent plantings. Now and again we attempted to ride up some short stretch, only to decide it was too like one of the more taxing mountain sections of the Tour de France. There was a vast ocean of trees on every hand, acre upon monotonous acre, and we thought the end to them would never come. Once a wren gave a passing greeting with a sudden burst of song, and higher a bullfinch family quartet encouraged us briefly for our final effort. Thankfully we paused to draw breath at the boundary fence. It was exactly midday.

We looked out now across the watershed moors where, in the distance, a dozen or so hinds were grazing. It was good to be free of the trees at last, although peaty puddles and heathery detours proved to be no kindly exchange for the forestry track. However, once in the narrows of the Lairig Chalbhath, we reckoned it would all be pleasantly plain sailing. From there on it would be downhill all the way, an amiable descent over the last kindly miles. Fondly we imagined it would be just like the familiar opening verses of Henry Charles Beeching's boy's song "Going down Hill on a Bicycle":

With lifted feet, hands still,
I am poised, and down the hill
Dart, with heedful mind;
The air goes by in a wind.

Swifter and yet more swift,
Till the heart with a mighty lift
Makes the lungs laugh, the throat cry:
'O bird, see; see, bird, I fly.'

In the event — as, of course, we should have foreseen — it was not quite like that. No bird-like swoop this, only a slow, painful progression from bump to interminable bump. In fact it was an almost exact repetition of the descent on our previous crossing: a sandy track of arm-juddering obstacles, rocks and ruts, potholes and puddles. But it *was* downhill. Success was assured. At last we were alongside the Allt a' Choire Uidhre on the familiar half mile to the haven of the Glen Lyon road.

We were in excellent time for the postbus pick-up and we sat back on a grassy bank gazing with drowsy satisfaction far into space. Like Tennyson's lotos-eaters we decided there could be nothing more delectable than

With half-shut eyes ever to seem
Falling asleep in a half-dream!

Then suddenly we were awake. The postbus had rounded the corner and was bearing down upon us. But it was no minibus, only an ordinary car. What, we wondered, would happen to our bicycles?

We need not have worried. The driver, Jim Macdonald, escorting us to the "big house"

Crossing the ford over the Shochie Burn near Little Glenshee farm.

near-by, had no difficulty in securing an out-house corner for our steeds; he himself would collect them for us once his minibus (temporarily out of order with faulty brakes) was on the road again. We sat back contentedly in the car to enjoy the run back down the glen.

And enjoy it we certainly did; not just the scenery, but the bits and pieces of Jim's own personal story. A dozen years on the Glen Lyon run "and every day different. The best occupation in Britain, for job satisfaction." Here was a social service of incalculable worth: collecting an old person's pension, paying for another's daily papers, even making soup once a week for an elderly cottager crippled with arthritis; simply keeping a watchful eye open for anyone in sudden, special need. There were numerous stories, macabre stories, adventure stories; stories of winter blizzards and drifts so deep that even the plough and blower were unable to cope. Material and more for a book which one day Jim must assuredly write. For us a journey not to be forgotten. Too soon over.

STAGE THREE of our journey had an attractive look about it, with the inclusion of two of the finest glens in Perthshire, Glen Lyon and Glen Lochay. Appropriately enough, it began in the Glen Lyon postbus. This time, as Jim Macdonald was on holiday, we were in the hands of relief driver Bob Cassidy. It was only Bob's third spell on the glen run and it would hardly have been surprising had he made a few even minor mistakes with his bewildering multitude of deliveries. He made none, and into the bargain he regaled us with interest enough to make his "social service" run into an epic to remember.

The stop-start six miles to Coshieville were the key to the journey ahead, the explanation of the 30 minutes shown on the timetable. Here and beyond in the glen itself morning papers were tossed dexterously into the roadside boxes. Often enough, too, there were milk deliveries to be made; at one cottage a prescription from the Aberfeldy chemist, at another a couple of library books. And often an apt enlivening comment: "We bring along odd things now and again; yesterday I had a live duck to deliver." Passing a solitary jogger, we were told "He's slower this morning; he was away along the road

yesterday." And at one of the boxes a slightly longer pause: "You have to wrap the papers here in a special way. The dog comes to fetch them and if you don't do them up properly he simply refuses to carry them up to the house." At one lonely cottage far up the glen the previous day's mail had not been uplifted; a check had to be made with the nearest neighbour to make sure that all was well.

We said good-bye to Bob and the postbus where the road drops finally to Lubreoch, below the Loch Lyon dam. The work of the day lay ahead.

Thinking frequent thoughts of our route beforehand, I had decided that the initial climb to the bealach at 1650 feet would be the most taxing part of our trip. In the event I was proved wrong. Partly because of the helpful start and remarkably gentle gradient, and partly because we were fresh, it all went with an ease that surprised us. The really hard part of the day was to come at the end, when the miles had become many times longer and every slight rise a challenge. In fact, the climb to the notch of the pass, the Lairig nan Lunn, took less than an hour and included a leisurely pause for lunch. It was a pleasant enough day — the forecast had been for bright intervals with a south-west or north-west breeze of 15 to 25 knots — and I decided we must have misheard a remark during a coffee-stop at Bridge of Balgie that it was snowing up on the tops. Actually the sun was breaking through in distant patches, catching beautifully the snow-cornice rimming the plateau of Beinn Achaladair. Nearer, the long eastern arm of Loch Lyon gave no hint of the look of the valley in the days before hydro-electric development — a bleak expanse of moorland with an unremarkable little loch no more than a mile and a half long. Past it occasionally would come, over the barrier ridge from Rannoch Moor, the drovers and their beasts, still with much weariness ahead of them on their long trail to the South.

Our own halt, after only a few minutes of uphill walking, was not exactly deserved, though none the less welcome. Near where we sat perched on a roadside bank, a meadow pipit kept climbing and parachuting cheerfully, and for further entertainment we heard occasionally the rippling music of a curlew down below us in the trough of the moorland burn.

The view north to Meall Buidhe from Stuchd an Lochain, above Glen Lyon.

I did not recognise the upper reaches of Glen Lochay. This was perhaps not altogether surprising: my only other visit had been at New Year in 1938. Four of us had been driven by a friend up the glen to Kenknock with the object of traversing Beinn Heasgarnich (3530 feet) and Creag Mhor (3387 feet). My yellowing diary tells me that it had been severe frost the previous night and that the road was icy — apparently of only minimal concern to our driver, who negotiated the fierce Glen Lochay bends with carefree abandon and deposited us not a little shaken at our destination. We had started by climbing by way of "a good path" to the top of the Lairig nan Lunn — evidently no motorable road in those days — then turned westwards over two miles of moorland to the long peat-hag ridge of Heasgarnich. On Creag Mhor, second Munro of the day, we had been rewarded with a superb winter sunset, but it was long after dark — black as the proverbial navvy's tea — before we reached glen levels again, the final miles to Auch and a pre-arranged lift round to Crianlarich.

On our way again, Mais and I pedalled a couple of miles down the glen, then stopped for another sandwich on the turf at the roadside. We were thoroughly well pleased with ourselves: everything so far had gone remarkably easily and we still felt full of energy. We smiled benignly at half a dozen sheep across the road, cropping the grassy bank at the river's edge; it mattered little that they remained singularly unimpressed.

Our self-congratulation lasted all the way to Killin. The road was gently downhill for most of the remaining six miles, with the wind a useful ally as well. The many peaty trout pools of the river, slow-moving below polished rock-faces,

The Lairig was typical of dozens in the Highlands, familiar and unfamiliar: bare and windswept, with nondescript heather slopes dropping to a narrow lochan. The latter was on the farther side of the watershed, mirroring the chill grey of the clouds. It was cold as we paused for a breather, with no escape from the teasing wind: too optimistic, we decided, to look for any bird life on the lochan. The only interest was a solitary ring ouzel chacking at us from the roadside, doubtless with recollections of kindlier warmth in North Africa only recently quitted.

The two-mile descent of almost 1000 feet had the pattern of a pass-storming epic in Norway. The road surface could not have been kinder, but the angle was relentlessly steep with sharp elbow bends, so that there was no relief from teeth gritted and fingers aching with endlessly clutching the brakes. The wind seemed degrees colder, too, as if straight from the snowfields 3000 feet above the head of Glen Lochay. We were not sorry to reach the levels of the farmland at Kenknock. The time was two o'clock, reassuringly within our schedule.

invited longer stops than we could afford. Some were half hidden by a profusion of hawthorn blossom bordering the road, while for more distant views we had unfamiliar glimpses of the wedge of the Tarmachan ridge.

Another ingredient added to the afternoon's mix of enjoyment was a detour to look at the Falls of Lochay. This was, of course, treading in the footsteps of not a few august visitors of the past: Charles Dickens, for example, who walked up the glen from Killin, was particularly appreciative. "It was a magnificent sight," he wrote afterwards, "foaming and crashing down three great steeps of riven rock, leaping over the first as far as you could carry your eye, and rumbling and foaming down into a dizzy pool below you, with a deafening roar." A description which we could hardly have bettered.

We reached the main road in commendably good order; another section of the journey had been completed. The warm glow of satisfaction was with us still.

And that — for half the party at least — was where the glow came to an end.

Travelling east from Killin by car — after the initial climb from Bridge of Lochay — it is scarcely noticeable that the road rises uphill at all. From behind the handlebars of a one-gear bicycle it is all very different: the way ahead looks thoroughly unfriendly and it is soon plain that it is going to continue uphill for ever. In fact it reminds one of nothing so much as the final slope of some undistinguished Munro, on which the summit cairn recedes further and further, the higher one plods, into an impossibly remote distance. Now and again, as we toiled upwards, I looked across Loch Tay hoping for some encouragement in the views, only to find myself speculating morosely on the effort that would no doubt be needed if we were to be so misguided as to continue our journey southward down the map at some later date. Passing the road-end below the Lawers visitor centre, I could not help reflecting on the trouble we might have been saved had we avoided going to the head of Glen Lyon at all and instead simply crossed over from Bridge of Balgie — a temptation to cheat which would, of course, have been much too unworthy ever to have crossed our minds. Fortunately Mais's thoughts were on an altogether loftier plane; her morale was still laudably high and she strove nobly with glucose

tablets and words of cheer to save me from ultimate depths of despair. At last, somehow, we reached the "summit". Before us stretched three miles of freewheeling to the haven of Fearnan — and Iain Campbell with his van.

In the event Iain, typically, came half of the way up the hill to meet us. Mais, I believe, would happily have pedalled on to Aberfeldy. My own enthusiasm was less in evidence. Iain, as a fellow conspirator so to speak, was much too kind to comment.

"THE TIME to stop trouble," remarked Para Handy to Dougie the mate, "iss before it starts." So I reflected for most of a sleepless night before the final stage of our cycle ride down the Perthshire map. The question which nagged me was quite simply whether I would in fact be able to complete the 26-mile switchback we had planned; if, as imagination suggested, we were to grind wearily to a halt at some particularly remote spot, how would we meet up with Iain Campbell and his van for the all-important homeward lift? All we could do was wait, with such patience as we could muster, and see.

Iain arrived at 7.30 precisely to sweep us — Mais, the bicycles and me — the four miles up the Crieff road from Aberfeldy to the far end of Loch na Craige. It was a morning that reminded me of Swiss mountain dawns: grey cloud-stippling and thin ribbons of ice-blue sky; the sun not far away. Some of the more distant hill-barriers were still part-shrouded in mist. Aloof, Schiehallion stood tall, majestically clear. We were in the middle of an unusually fine weather spell in early September; even the T.V. met. men had conceded that there might be sunshine over the Central Highlands. Four days before, from high on the quartz spine of Schiehallion, we had gazed far over the smoke blue of the nearer Grampians. There had been no more than a light touch of wind; it had looked permanently set fair.

"Great," I observed to Iain as he lifted our machines for us over the fence and on to the familiar forestry track. "The only snag is I'm not sure if I can make it all the way to Buchanty."

"Well, you've managed to survive every time so far," Iain answered. "And anyway, I'll be passing back by Kinloch at midday. That would be roughly half way for you, so you can pack in then if you like." It was the answer to our problem of the previous evening. Had I known, I might have slept the night through without a hint of worry.

Mais and I started slowly up the brae. We felt in surprisingly good form. It was good to feel free with a whole long day stretching before us. We paid no heed to a startled grouse which advised us emphatically to go back. Meadow pipits, first of many, flirped away from the fringe of the track. Somewhere in the sitkas a wren chattered a machine-gun scolding as we passed.

We had expected to feel leaden-footed on the first gradients of the day; in fact they troubled us remarkably little, warming us up — most acceptably, indeed, as there was still an early chill in the air. Almost unexpectedly we were in sight of Loch Kennard, hustling now to reach the long free-wheel sections we knew should lie ahead. Before that we were rewarded twice — first with a picture-view over the loch which was new to us, then with a rest for self-congratulation on a heathery bank 3½ miles from take-off point.

The long, gradual descent went to our heads like champagne. The track surface was firm and even, so that a mere score of yards had us wanting to sing for sheer *joie de vivre*. This surely was what hill-track cycling was all about: uphill plodding, soggy sand-ruts, upthrust boulders — all forgotten in one glorious swoop.

Almost two miles of it, a straight open stretch, then a gentle left-handed swing still vaguely downhill, and we were pausing again where the track crossed the Pitleoch Burn. Here was a cluster of hardwood plantings — good to see, as were the open boundaries to much of the track now climbing beyond. It was surprisingly still: no wind, only silence and complete peace as we looked out over the feather-tops of the sitkas.

Unexpectedly the track began to deteriorate; only slightly, but enough to cause a vague feeling of unease. Then suddenly, with no more warning, we were emphatically at the end of the line — an open turning-point hemmed in all round by a barrier of trees with a depressingly impenetrable look. Immediate reactions were not altogether surprising: we were high on the hill overlooking Trochry and the stretch of main road there which we had somehow to reach; the steep slopes in between, so far as we could make out beyond the immediate screening

conifers, were generously covered in whins and broom; our first, hasty inspection disclosed no possible way of escape. Where, we wondered, did we go from there?

Then, second time round, we found the answer: an immovable rusty gate, half-hidden in a tangle of undergrowth, barring the way to a path buried in knee-high grass. Heaving the cycles over, we embarked on the steep descent which earlier we had imagined would be another free-wheel delight. After a few yards the jungle grass gave way to ruts, boulders and bumps hemmed in tightly by the whins and broom. Where we were able to ride, our concentration and hard braking suggested a way down like the back of some remote Munro, guaranteed to rattle the most resilient skeleton. Fortunately the frames of our very ordinary machines stood up to the punishment without complaint.

At Trochry our watches said 10.10. We had come 9½ miles. After the pummelling we had been suffering, the main road seemed laughably friendly. However, the next turn-off — another 3¼ miles on and roughly the halfway mark — was mildly uphill. The sun broke through aggressively hot. Excuses, like straws, had to be clutched: five minutes for squash and glucose; a word or two with an elderly English walker; go-slows to watch the "tattie-howkers" bent double over the shaws, scooping the potatoes into their tubs; even a pause to turn back to safety a "hairy jock" caterpillar heading for certain destruction in a purposeful sortie across the road.

At the signpost indicating the footpath to Little Glenshee temptation loomed large. It was here, if we chose, that we could call it a day, pedal along to Kinloch and return to Aberfeldy with Iain, homeward bound on his midday business.

"How about it?" I asked Mais.

It was a stupid question, and we knew it. If anyone had suggested we were flagging, our indignation would have known no bounds. We were delighted with our performance so far. And anyway we were actually four minutes ahead of schedule.

A dip and sharp climb beyond had us quickly past the old stone bridge over the Braan. Here we were no longer on a sandy forestry track, but, strangely, on rather unfriendly slate. It was a long upward slog, although we were thankful to be still in good enough trim to be able to savour fully the magnificence of the day. The principal joy was that we were now out on open moorland — sheer delight after the monotonous sitka deserts of the morning. There was nothing dramatic about the views, only a sense of boundless freedom, reaching away to the vague blue horizon; but it was open landscape at its best and we sent a mental vote of thanks to the landowner for having withstood the temptation to put beauty up for sale in exchange for yet another sad, sad desolation of conifers.

For a while the slate of the track gave way to sand, but unfortunately that was too friendly to last. Opposite the deserted farm of Rosecraig, at rather more than 1000 feet, it began to degenerate, telling us all too clearly what lay ahead. We were over the watershed and so starting to descend; but it was to be no free-wheel holiday yet awhile. With bushy, bristling growth down the centre, the ruts on either side were hard to see and harder to negotiate, so that we lurched and bounced along in perilously drunken slow motion. Soon, however, we were well into the throat of Glen Shee and a lunch-time halt was called for. What more pleasant than a heather bank and the sun almost too hot for comfort? Earlier we had watched a pair of buzzards effortlessly working the thermals high overhead; now in turn a pair of ravens grunted a greeting. The only irritation was provided by a mob of local midges surprisingly seizing the chance of an unexpectedly luscious variation to their normal lunch menu.

The struggle with the track lasted all the way to Little Glenshee farm. There abruptly, beyond a final gate, we left desolation and solitude behind. A sheepdog with four lively puppies, each a black and white replica of herself, warned us off with harsh salvos of sound and fury. Taking not the slightest bit of interest, an elderly billy goat continued to look down his splendidly patrician nose, chomping the while a totally disdainful cud. We were back in civilisation.

Carefree as the old goat himself, we dropped in an exultant free-wheel to a well-engineered ford through the Shochie Burn, then climbed round the corner of a wood to three miles of genteel, slightly downhill pedalling and a magnificent stretch of mixed woodland.

The last miles of the day, to Buchanty, proclaiming everywhere the tidiness of harvest-home and orderly, prosperous gardens, might well have been pure anti-climax, had it not been for two things. The first was a welcome — maybe even well-earned — cup of tea with good friends in Harrietfield. The second, quite simply, was our meeting up with Iain. He and the van appeared half a mile on the way to meet us, on schedule to the minute. It was particularly fitting that he should have been in on the last act just as he had been in so importantly on the first, all those many weeks back and all those many miles away at Dalnaspidal, as we headed into the storm-force wind along the track past Loch Garry, into the heather gateway to the South.

Glen Lyon

The river is a foam-flecked horse
Bred fleet. Above, there is a flinching of doves,
Making a windmill of the sun.
Autumn, leaving his oils and brushes
Bathes bare feet in the deep pools.
A salmon browses through shallows
Nudging the upturned hills of the mirror,
Nipping a fly. In the high corries
The first few wolves of snow have gone to sleep
And the rowans are speaking of storm.

Outstanding birdwatching country: Taymouth Castle woods and Drummond Hill.

ENJOYING A CENTURY OF BIRDS

Voices

The woodpecker taps out morse
Crows scrawl arguing across dawn in German.

Woodpigeons make soft French love words
As little twigs of sparrows chatter in Italian.

The raven is Norse, his voice chipped from sharp cliffs
And geese squabble over Icelandic sagas.

In the middle of winter all I hear are the curlews
Crying at night their Gaelic laments.

FOR THE ordinary, enthusiastic, reasonably energetic, moderately skilled bird-watcher the game of trying to see a hundred different species in a month is not particularly difficult. From the *machair* of the islands to the uptilted moors of Drumochter, from the pine-woods of Speyside to estuaries such as Ythan or Eden, the scope is virtually unlimited. Indeed the utterly dedicated will notch up his century not in a leisurely month but in a single day — after all, at the time of writing the one-day record is reported to stand at an almost unbelievable 134. Yet humbler mortals, probably with not over-much leisure time to spare, may find that even with a month to play with, the contest is apt to turn out to be a close-run thing.

My own experiences call for no wild shouts of acclamation. In 1976, for example, when we were living in the West of Scotland, we had reached 31st May with a single sighting still needed for the century. Daylight was beginning to fade and hope had dwindled to a flicker. Then, suddenly, from our next-door neighbours' roof-top an all-white bird flew down — an albino starling.

The total I allowed myself was 99·5.

Complete success came not very long afterwards. In spite of a move to Perthshire and consequently less familiar hunting-grounds, there were actually two memorable years when the target was reached. Yet both of these were for the whole of Scotland, and the more I thought about it, the more convinced I became that this was really too easy: the rules should be tightened to limit the contest to Perthshire only. This, of course, would put an entirely different complexion on the challenge. For one thing, without any real coastline, approximately ten species would be wiped at a stroke from the list of "possibles" — a fact which became only too clear when the idea was put into practice and year after year failure continued to succeed failure. The nearest I could come to the revised target was a score of 96. Clearly a much more imaginative strategy was essential. Like doing the Macnab or climbing all the Munros, a deal of hard work seemed to be called for: some good solid homework beforehand and more sustained effort throughout the month itself.

It was easy enough to make a list: on paper the century did not look too formidable. It was obvious, however, that in the higher flights, so to speak, a good deal of luck was always necessary, so I chose a number of additional "five stars" which were not completely impossible and which might help to fill any troublesome gaps.

The chosen month was, of course, May — indisputably the best time of year for putting in the attack. "Early May," observes Viscount Grey of Fallodon in *The Charm of Birds*, "is the one period of the season when all our birds are present and most visible. Before this, though the trees are bare, the stock of birds is incomplete: later the thick summer growth of leaves and herbage hides them." In Scotland this spell when conditions are ideal can certainly seem cruelly brief: one can decide easily enough that the month's initial welcome is too bleak and inhospitable for the migrants, yet only a few days later have a feeling akin to panic as one sees the trees burgeoning fast in a sudden burst of summer warmth.

In 1989, sundry other ideas came crowding in to enliven the days before May arrived: excellent intentions (never fulfilled) to go into training for scouring the high tops for dotterel and

Peewits' nest near Loch Moraig, Blair Atholl.

ptarmigan; practice in early rising (certainly never carried out) for surprising capercaillies among the pines topping Drummond Hill; attempts in April (completely unsuccessful) to pinpoint the whereabouts of golden eagles, hen-harriers and woodpeckers; the study of old Perthshire bird reports (too out of date to be other than merely tantalising). I planned innumerable attractive-looking outings and consulted the tide-tables for the Tay estuary in order to come up with the best timing for visits to the mudflats at Invergowrie. In addition my ears were tuned in to the occasional titbits of bird-watching gossip, although I hesitated to ask some unsuspecting acquaintances the location of a certain estate near Perth; it seemed much too embarrassing to have to explain that what I was really wanting to know was precisely where the Tay mandarin ducks disappeared to during the nesting season.

And so the last weeks and days slipped past . . .

"May 1st. Wakened while it was still dark and lay hoping for a good dawn chorus. Eventually a solitary blackbird started a half-hearted solo, then, lacking support, gave up and returned disheartened to his couch. Reckon the local cats must be putting a damper on any performance near the house. I could hear better music in the distance; faint, but a full-throated chorus."

So ran the first of my May Day diary jottings.

We were up and away by 6.30. It was dull and damp, with mist trailing along the higher ridges. For better, for worse, the contest was on.

Each year our May Day programme follows the same traditional pattern: out from Aberfeldy to Coshieville; up past Glengoulandie deer farm to Loch Kinardochy and the Schiehallion road to Kinloch Rannoch; home then to breakfast by Dunalastair and Tummel Bridge. A pleasant round of 38 miles, full of possibilities.

As usual it started predictably enough: no cruising osprey, no sudden flash of kingfisher blue past the Tay bridge; just very ordinary, everyday sightings. Then, a brief hint of encouragement — a goldfinch, startled to a roadside perch just past the Dull turn-off. Above the gorge of the Keltney Burn Mais played momentary havoc with the morning's harmony by seeing a pair of jays — which I missed. She kindly offered not to count them, a gesture which fortunately went for nought, as we had another view of one during the homeward run. Loch Kinardochy, first loch of the day and normally to be relied on for a useful contribution or two, was disappointingly birdless apart from its small colony of common gulls, restless and peevish as usual.

However, we hoped for better things as we approached little Loch an Daimh, unrippled in the shelter of its reed-fringed saucer, wondering in particular if the solitary whooper swan would be there to greet us once again. In each May of the three preceding years he (or she) had been there, always on his own — an intriguing puzzle. Was it, we questioned, injury or choice or even some curious form of whooper ostracism which had caused this separation from the main herd elsewhere? Surely this time it just wouldn't happen again: surely he would be away with the others to their wilderness haunt in Iceland. But we were wrong. There he was, scarcely ten yards from the road, dirty indeed with dabbling in the depths of the reed-bed, but dignified, stately, superbly unconcerned. Four days later, when we passed that way again, there was no sign of him.

In parenthesis, this whooper story has a particularly fascinating sequel. In May of the following year, when we visited Loch an Daimh as usual, we were thrilled to find not just a lonely single, but a pair of birds in residence. We could scarcely believe our eyes; we hardly dared hope for things to come. But we were not to be disappointed. When we returned later in the month, one of the whoopers, half-hidden in an island thicket of reeds, was sitting, clearly on the nest. An appropriate few weeks after, there — where weeds and open water met — were the proud parents up-ending and dabbling for four healthy-looking cygnets. Perthshire history had been made; we had been privileged indeed. (According to the British Trust for Ornithology *Atlas*,* "Less than half a dozen cases of breeding are known in this century.")

To return to Day One in the tale of our century bid, as we left Loch an Daimh the sky was blueing up steadily and by the time we had reached Kinloch Rannoch the sun was out, giving added sparkle to show after show of daffodils. A detour along the lochside was unrewarding, merely tempting us with the idea of stopping for a bar breakfast: a bacon roll and a mug or two of tea would certainly not have gone amiss. But along beside Dunalastair reservoir there were other, better things to catch our attention: a tree pipit exuberantly vocal, a hoodie and a carrion crow fraternising on the road, several small groups of greylags still not away on the long miles to Iceland; on the loch itself a female goldeneye, tufties in plenty, a few wary wigeon, a heron half-hidden in distant reeds, grey as a bleached tree-skeleton. Before we reached Tummel Bridge we had filled two or three more gaps in the list; near Glengoulandie once again, we had a face-to-face confrontation with a kestrel, bright-hued as autumn bracken, perched almost within touching distance on a fence-post. Home and breakfast at last, and so, with a few "domestic" additions in the afternoon, to the end of the day and a total of 38.

A necessary journey to Perth on 2nd May gave us the chance of one of our traditional forays on the North Inch beside the Tay. A county cricket match in progress gave an added touch of summer to a day of pleasantly warm sunblinks. The Tay itself, with a flickering of sand martins and mallards in plenty (nine ducklings in one family party) had an unusually benevolent look about it. Several merganser pairs and a solitary goosander drake with three redheads in attendance were enjoying their feeding close under the further bank, while the familiar gaunt guano-white roosting tree (at that time still standing) had its quota of cormorant tenants, perched like a gang of scrawny vultures hungry for carrion.

Our route home to Aberfeldy took us through the Sma' Glen, and during a pause there our attention was caught by the "kronking" of a pair of ravens, eastbound high above us. They were the only ones we were to see during the whole month, and I found it interesting to be told later by Martin Robinson, warden at the R.S.P.B. Balrobbie reserve, at Killiecrankie, that in his opinion ravens in Perthshire are nowadays less common even than peregrines. This is an observation borne out by Miss Valerie M. Thom in her fine book *Birds in Scotland*†. Of the raven she says: "Still widely distributed in the Highlands and islands but has decreased markedly in central Scotland and the Southern Uplands since the 1950s, especially in areas where there has been extensive afforestation." And by comparison: "The Peregrine's status in the mid 1980s is more encouraging than it has been for many years. In some grouse moor areas of eastern Scotland more Peregrines are breeding than were ever recorded previously."

Next morning warm sun and a cloudless sky gave the kind of promise to guarantee perfection at Loch Meallbrodden. The half-mile approach there along the moorland track above Fowlis Wester is a treat on no account to be missed; the lark-song alone is virtually continuous (we called it "the day of the larks"), one soloist after another taking up the refrain, with constant rivalry from peewits, curlews and meadow pipits. An extra bonus — one in fact for which we had been hoping in particular — was the sight of a pair of golden plovers, strikingly handsome as always, posing on heather lookouts not a dozen yards from the sandy, rutted track. On the loch itself a boat was out, but as

---

* *The Atlas of Breeding Birds in Britain and Ireland. J.T.R. Sharrock. (T.& A.D. Poyser. 1976.)*

† T. & A.D. Poyser Ltd (1986).

expected we glimpsed one of the Canada goose family always in residence, along with the usual tufties and coots. At a distant corner of the rushes a redshank pair took a long-range dislike to our presence.

Earlier, on the road, we had passed a *coileach dubh* — or, more familiarly, a blackcock — so close at the verge that I could easily have stopped the car, leaned out and tickled his lyre tail. Among the Loch Meallbrodden heather, too, we had put up quite a number of red grouse — maybe nothing remarkable in that, yet always a pleasant reminder that the "sportsmen" still haven't had the final word, that muirfowl are not yet quite extinct. Back in 1920, when the eastern portion of the Breadalbane sporting and agricultural estates, including Taymouth Castle, were put up for auction in London by Knight, Frank & Rutley, the shootings on the various lots were claimed to have averaged 2105 brace of grouse over the preceding eight years. In 1912 the bag on the Moness estate of 8400 acres, the most prolific, had been no less than 2858 brace, a statistic not easy to credit today when one hears the startled "go back, go back" of occasional startled stragglers.

In the past, two hopeful visits to Stormont Loch, the Scottish Wildlife Trust reserve two miles south of Blairgowrie, had not come up to expectations. On the first occasion the loch had quite simply been frozen solid; on the second, it might as well have been ice-bound again for all the ornithological good things it provided for us. We hoped, for our third visit, that it would do better.

In the event we had only moderate good fortune. At the hide itself a telescope would have been helpful, with the waterfowl plentiful enough, but mostly favouring the far shore. A pair of great crested grebes were obligingly obvious, as also — much more surprisingly — were a pair of pochard ("five stars" at last). We could have wished for a more impressive day's total, although a passing glimpse of some stock doves — more easily seen in that eastern part of the county — and a short-eared owl drifting over the moor nearer home were additions in the by-going not to be despised.

The following afternoon a westward journey introduced a fresh contrast. In my earlier

Whooper swan family group, Loch an Daimh. (**John Wiseman**)

Cock bullfinch, a none-too-welcome fruit tree visitor. (**Meg Dunn**)

"homework" I had come across an interesting snippet in the British Trust for Ornithology *Atlas* which turned my thoughts to another truly worth-while "five star", a greenshank. According to this information, a favoured nesting area was near the old snow-fencing alongside the West Highland railway, and it seemed to me that all we had to do to score another useful point was to walk along the line where it crosses Rannoch Moor. We went therefore to spend the night at the Moor of Rannoch Hotel, meeting up there with our son Kenneth, who travelled up from Glasgow.

As usual, however, things worked out differently in that little way they have. We saw no greenshanks. But we were rewarded otherwise. In the gloaming after dinner we heard several snipe drumming and although we failed to spot one, we watched two the following morning quite close to the hotel and I even found a nest "in four". There was, however, more — much more — to that morning's enjoyment. The views out across the wilderness of the Moor to the Bridge of Orchy and Blackmount Munros, snow-ribbed, startlingly brilliant in the stark clarity

of early sunlight, were quite breathtaking. They were with us all the way on our railway line sortie and as we cut across the heather to that lovely arc of sand at the head of Loch Laidon. And there at the water's edge, welcoming us with his plaintive "tlui", was a ringed plover. Rich rewards indeed.

The journey home, in hot sunshine, was uneventful. Yet, not having been for some time in that western corner of the county, we were struck afresh by the moonscape look of the scenery between Rannoch station and Bridge of Gaur: wild, rock-littered foreground and background of far distant snow-brindled hills; all reminiscent of the remote lava hinterland of Iceland.

The next day, 7th May, was not particularly noteworthy. In fact, it sounds downright dull to say that the best thing about it was that we came on a pair of long-tailed tits among the scattered moorland birches up above Kenmore. Yet, although we see these tits often enough in winter when they are noisily *en famille*, they never seem to be nearly so obliging — for us at least — during the breeding season, so that a sighting then is always especially welcome. They are, of course, particularly engaging little birds and it is hardly surprising that they should have attractive characters to match. For example, writing nearly a century ago, Richard Kearton observed that all the other tits hiss aggressively like snakes when disturbed on their nests, the marsh tit even managing to bite as well; not so the "longties", maybe because they are so snug in their 2000-feather downies where, incidentally, the male sensibly keeps the female company at night during the period of brooding. They are indeed real family birds, always happily together on the move and said to sleep touching each other in a row, perched on a branch. Some of their dozen and more local names — such as "poke-pudding" or "long-pod" — have a touch of the ridiculous and show something of the affection in which they are held. Perhaps "oven-builder" is as expressive as any; it must be warm to say the least while a round dozen youngsters are sleeping snugly cheek to cheek. At least in their early days their tails are conveniently short.

There was one other good thing about the day of the long-tailed tits and that was that it was then that the swifts arrived: typically, of course — one moment nothing, then suddenly skimming the town's rooftops; welcome back, as always, and slightly earlier than the average arrival date I had worked out over the preceding eight years — 10th May. I am sure they must have known what kind of weather we were having: yet another day of lavish sunshine. One wonders indeed if swifts do delay their arrival until the weather is suitably warm for them. In this connection an old bird book of 1909, *British Birds in their Haunts*, by the Rev.C.A. Johns, has some interesting comments to make on the effects of abnormally cold weather:

With respect to temperature, the swift's powers of endurance are limited; it never proceeds far northwards, and occasionally even suffers from unseasonably severe weather in the temperate climates where it fixes its summer residence. Mr F. Smith, of the British Museum, related in the *Zoologist* that, at Deal, on the eighth of July, 1856, after a mild but wet day, the temperature suddenly fell till it became disagreeably cold. The swifts were sensibly affected by the atmospheric change; they flew unsteadily, fluttered against the walls of the houses, and some even flew into open windows. "Whilst observing these occurrences", he says, "a girl came to the door to ask me if I wanted to buy a bat; she had heard, she told me, that I bought all kinds of bugs, and her mother thought I might want a bat. On her producing it, I was astonished to find it was a poor benumbed swift. The girl told me they were dropping down in the streets; the church, she said, was covered with them. Off I started to witness this strange sight. True enough; on arriving at the church in Lower Street I was astonished to see the poor birds hanging in clusters from the eaves and cornices; some clusters were at least two feet in length, and, at intervals, benumbed individuals dropped from the outside of the clusters."

Sad contrast indeed to warm wintering in southern Africa.

Next morning an unexpected weather change to sullen skies and a teasing wind ushered in five days of low morale, one of those spells which intrude inevitably after the first flush of enthusiasm is past. A pair of reed buntings in marshland near Loch Freuchie, the first of the usually numerous garden warblers, and a sparrowhawk, purposeful as a low-flying jet, were three of seven additions to the list. Most cheering of the septet, however, was a roding woodcock, heard and then seen above the familiar clearing in "our" wood beside the Crieff road. From viewings in previous years, we had worked out beforehand his estimated time of appearance and decided that it should be 9.52 p.m. precisely. Something, however, must have delayed the start of his evening round; he did not show up until 10.12, heralded by his customary mouse-squeaks and growl.

Much less satisfying was the green woodpecker. We had heard a tantalising amount of "yaffling" coming from the untidy woodland jungle which reaches round the face of Weem rock; we had even paid two visits, both of which ended merely in frustration. The third attempt to spot the woodpecker was only slightly better: Mais did have a reasonable glimpse of our quarry; mine, sadly, was more a matter of hearsay. The result was one of those tough battles of conscience which are apt to occur every now and again, when it is best to take refuge in the old adage: "I used to be undecided; now I'm not so sure."

The way in which the green woodpecker has extended its range into and through Scotland is a truly remarkable success story. In the old *Statistical Account* of the 1790s there are a number of references to woodpeckers, though only one, so far as could be discovered, specifically to the green — appropriately enough in the parish of Dunkeld. In the account of the parish of Birse, in South-west Aberdeenshire, there is mention of "woodpeckers of the larger and lesser kinds" and in Strichen, also in Aberdeenshire, of "different kinds of woodpeckers." Intriguing, but sadly helping little towards corroborating the Dunkeld mention. Much later, in 1908, Richard Kearton noted: "The green woodpecker does not breed in either Scotland or Ireland," and it was not until the 1920s that there was the first official record of it — in Perthshire. Even then it was only in 1967 that breeding there was first proved. Now it is well and truly established. Quite apart from the Aberfeldy area we have had several sightings in and near Crieff in past years — for example, at the "back" of the Knock and beside the road up to Loch Turret — and later in our 1989 wanderings we were to hear still more "yaffling" in the fine mixed woodland above Killiecrankie.

On 13th May we were back to the sunshine which was to make the summer of 1989 so memorable, and we were encouraged accordingly. It was what I sometimes think of as "greenfinch weather," one of those warm, sunny mornings when the "greenies" simply cannot stop bubbling over with exuberant *joie de vivre*. Keenly looked forward to, the day's programme was a visit to Invergowrie and neighbourhood, fringing the Tay estuary — Perthshire's "seaside". Much previous calculation to work out the state of the tide miraculously turned out to be accurate: we arrived, as hoped for, at approximately half ebb. And there with a welcome — not unexpected — was a pair of shelduck, the first of many we were to see afloat and on the mudflats. Apart, however, from distant shags and an immature herring gull (definitely not a bird to be seen in the heart of Perthshire), the Firth itself provided nothing more of interest. There were better things round about: in the farmhouse lanes linnets, goldfinches, whitethroats; in the reed-beds so many sedge warblers serenading the May morning that ordinary conversation seemed of singularly little consequence.

Drummond Hill two days later was just as noisy, with keen vocal competition among the warblers; only a chiffchaff, quieter than the others, kept annoyingly out of sight in its usual territory of crowded birches and rhododendrons. It was only when we climbed higher that we were properly rewarded, a family of siskins coming within feet for quite a confidential chat. That made 90 on the scoreboard. With half the month still to go, we felt quietly confident, even if it would perhaps be unfortunate to remark that by then we were counting our chickens.

It should perhaps be said at this point that included in our score were two birds not yet mentioned — a peregrine pair and a pair of black-throated divers. Their whereabouts must remain closely guarded secrets. Even a particularly inquisitive mole must be satisfied with the brief answer, "somewhere in Perthshire".

The Scottish Wildlife Trust's observation hide at the Loch of the Lowes was still on our agenda. So far we had had no news of how the ospreys were behaving, whether or not they had decided to set up house and home for the special benefit of visitors. We decided therefore that we had better go to find out for ourselves. As we took the road over to Dunkeld, battle raged between optimists and pessimists. Sadly the pessimists won. We were told that most days there had been sightings of birds over the loch, but that they had just never got down to the serious business of breeding. And as if further evidence was needed, we found the hide binoculars trained disconsolately on a very empty nest.

It was in May 1969 that the Loch of the Lowes reserve was acquired by the Scottish Wildlife Trust — not because of the ospreys, but on account of the area's rich and varied natural history interest. Most obligingly, however, a pair of ospreys did arrive in the following spring and although disaster overtook them when their nest was blown down in a fierce gale, they returned in 1971 and reared two healthy youngsters. Over the years since then — although latterly less dependable — the ospreys have continued to delight many thousands of visitors to the Trust's centre and hide, contributing to a significant extent to Scotland's most important ornithological story.

It would be surprising nevertheless if the Loch of the Lowes had been the only place in Perthshire to be favoured by returning ospreys. Back in the old days there were several well-recognised sites: for example, at the Lake of Menteith even as late as the 1840s, beside the priory on Inchmahome. There were eyries on Loch Tay and on Loch Ordie, above Dunkeld, the birds from the latter site probably being those mentioned in the old *Statistical Account* of two centuries ago as fishing occasionally in Loch Clunie, six miles away near Blairgowrie. Loch Ard in the parish of Aberfoyle used to be visited by the osprey pair which nested in the castle ruins on the Loch Lomond island of Inch Galbraith, while not to be outdone, the writer of the parish of Callander report remarks in his description of Loch Katrine: "On one side, the water eagle sits in majesty, undisturbed, on his well-known rock, in sight of his nest on the face of Ben Venue." Despite these old-time hints, however, supplemented by our own past experiences, we were not to have the pleasure of an osprey sighting during our century bid. This was particularly frustrating in a year (1989) when the overall total for Scotland was of 52 pairs of ospreys rearing more than 80 young, said to be the best figures for more than a century.

Quite apart from the non-present osprey pair, the day at the Lowes was disappointing. We walked up the dusty track to the Mill Dam, hoping to see a teal in the reedy nesting territory of the blackheaded gulls. We had no good fortune, however, only imprecations from the screaming cloud of inhabitants. We retreated, only just saving the day from complete ignominy by watching a spotted flycatcher insect-chasing from an oak tree down by the lochside. I could not help wondering if this particular flycatcher had any inkling of the amount of work in store for him and his wife once their brood had hatched. According to one keen observer, the Rev.C.A. Johns has noted*, "a pair of birds which he watched fed their young no less than five hundred and thirty-seven times in one day, beginning at twenty-five minutes before four o'clock in the morning, and ending at ten minutes before nine in the evening."

With relatively few likely sightings left for the latter part of the month, it is always difficult to keep morale from taking a tumble. Thus on the 17th, with the score-sheet lacking nine,

In upper Glen Almond, good territory for cuckoos and ring-ouzels.

* *British Birds in their Haunts (1909).*

we sallied forth intent on spotting a golden eagle. It was a long shot, a forlorn effort, in keeping with the grey cold of the morning up on the high moorland above Kenmore. And, needless to say, it failed. Instead we were almost ashamed to enjoy scoring quite so commonplace an alternative as a cuckoo. (We watched a pair chasing each other at 30 yards' range). We had heard several now and again a full fortnight earlier, but not one of these had come within viewing range.

Inevitably as the days pass there are the occasional doubtful sightings, the quick glimpses which one knows deep down are perfectly valid, yet which leave just enough of a question-mark to start a bitter battle with one's conscience. This means, if possible, "going over in ink" the most nagging queries. Such had been my Weem green woodpecker — counted for sure, but not double-checked. For the rest of the month it remained nothing more than an occasional far-off "yaffle". Not so my moorhen, glimpsed so poorly on Day 5 that it certainly required an "inking". Rather surprisingly this happened when we were looking for magpies. These are occasionally seen near Gleneagles, and we had gone scouting there with hopes high. We saw none. But across one of the immaculate lawns not far from the imposing front door of the hotel a moorhen jerked his supercilious way towards the bank of an adjacent lake. Honour was indeed satisfied.

With only eight sightings to go and 14 days left, we seemed to be in an unassailable position. When, too, a totally unexpected blackcap tried a snatch or two of song from a prominent roadside perch beside Weem Hotel and a walk up past Duireaskin was enlivened by the usual accompaniment of whinchats, things looked even better. We knew well enough, however, that it is with the final one or two that the acid test comes. We did not imagine that there would be any real need to try for the scoter family we heard tell of in one northern corner of the county, or to scour the Drumochter plateaux for dotterel, but we were pessimistic enough to wonder.

In fact, the next four came remarkably easily. Two separate tawny owls, disturbed during their afternoon siestas in the pines near Loch Kennard, were no doubt aggrieved at becoming mere ticks on a list. Some lesser black-backed gulls, normally seen without trouble near Crieff but less frequent visitors to Aberfeldy, were a useful bonus just within the county boundary on a heatwave journey to Edinburgh. On another superb afternoon we surprised a teal, last of the expected ducks, from a moorland puddle-chain up near Loch Derculich. On the steep west side of the Sma' Glen, from one of the slabby gullies of the uptilted boulder field, a pair of ring ouzels took off at extreme range, after much irascible chacking. We were at 98. Two, a mere two, to go.

Then for an entire week our skills deserted us.

One valuable day was both immensely enjoyable and a big disappointment. We went over to the R.S.P.B. Killiecrankie reserve for a walkabout with the warden, Martin Robinson. It was a grey morning: mist was trailing across the hunched nearest shoulder of Beinn a 'Ghlo, but there was no rain, only a touch of wind and not the flimsiest excuse for poor viewing. We had not previously visited the reserve and hopes were high as Martin emerged from the farm at Balrobbie to lead us off on our morning tour. A good tour it was, too, through woodland as magnificent surely as any in the county. I remember few details of our route — the path was pleasantly bewildering, following different levels high above the gorge of the Garry; never even mildly tedious, it allowed a real buzzard's eye view of much of the tree canopy, seeming at times like looking down into the green depths of some tropical rain forest. We were hoping in particular for two sightings, both — we optimistically imagined — so easy as to be almost cheating; a great spotted woodpecker and a pied flycatcher. They would, we agreed, make a quick, honourable climax to our century bid: Martin would lead us unerringly to a woodpecker's nesting hole and find at least one flycatcher pair at home in one of the numbered boxes known to house families. Not a bit of it. An area usually frequented by woodpeckers proved to be temporarily deserted and silent, while the flycatchers — normally noted accurately in their various boxes — had for once gone un-recorded, as the Balrobbie team had been too busy preparing for a forthcoming "open day". We heard several indeed, singing from the thickest foliage just to tantalise us, but not one deigning to allow us a glimpse. It was nevertheless a memorable round, with sightings such as redstarts and treecreepers which would have been possibly useful for our scoring earlier in the month. We even saw a cormorant heading hard for somewhere high overhead — a "first" for Balrobbie, Martin told us.

But we were still left with our elusive two.

After the sullen skies of the Killiecrankie morning spendthrift sunshine was back with us once more. The temptation was to take the chance of going for ptarmigan or even dotterel on the high tops, a brief interlude away from the woods. However, better judgement, or possibly merely laziness took us to the river instead. Somewhere on the shingle banks of the Tay a few pairs of common terns would be nesting; the trouble was to find them. Earlier in the month we had fitted in a brief recce near Meikleour where the river makes a big loop round the marshland of the Bloody Inches and where we had been told there might be a few pairs. However, we had drawn a blank, either because

the birds had still not arrived, or, more likely, because we were looking in the wrong place. Now I tried the Ballinluig islands and then some likely shingle spits beside the A9, three miles north of Dunkeld. I had a delightful, lazy hour or two of bird-watching — with one idyllic family scene when a merganser redhead emerged from under the bank and made off across the Tay with her seven chicks riding contentedly on her back — but not even a far glimpse of a tern.

Just to make matters that little bit worse, I stupidly wasted all of the following, valuable, morning in a wood not far from home which someone had kindly assured us was "full of woodpeckers". Unfortunately this happy state of affairs was clearly not appreciated by the birds themselves: I heard and saw none.

Things were now taking on a slightly desperate look. Admittedly four days remained, but if our rather feeble failures were to be allowed to continue, time was going to run out with the score at a not very creditable 98.

Dipper and sandpiper habitat: the shore of Loch Rannoch.

Just how concerned we were may be judged by the solemn fact that the next morning we were up at four o'clock. Things had to be really serious for us to have reached such a pass: we were gambling on seeing a capercaillie in the pines at the top of Drummond Hill. It was chilly and uninspiring as we set off, and the particularly vocal warblers beside the first stretches of path seemed almost obnoxiously cheerful. However, as we climbed higher and gradually shook off our lethargy, we had to admit that they might perhaps be right. A pair of bullfinches flew up from the track ahead; a robin was just too quick in making off to allow us to spot its nest; on the highest tip of a gaunt dead elm a tree pipit proclaimed greeting after greeting to the new day. Then we were among the conifers and the track climbed more roughly upwards. Our talk, such as it was, gave way to whispers and we trod more delicately on sandy patches and grass. Beyond the spruces the first of the pines began. And suddenly, with the violence of an exploding grenade, a caper burst from the upper branches of a tree a dozen yards ahead of us and flew arrow-straight away to fresh sanctuary in the depths of the wood. Satisfied, delighted, we turned and tramped contentedly down the long track back to the car.

One still to go: an intriguing question-mark. We simply had to succeed now. And, as usually happens, the answer was completely unexpected.

We were on our way the following evening to an engagement at Greenloaning. There seemed to be singularly little promise in that, unless, nearing journey's end, we were to be favoured by a kindly kingfisher on a bank of Allan Water. We did make a detour past Gleneagles, once again hoping that we might perhaps surprise a magpie foraging for a cast-off tiara in one of the hotel dustbins. Of course, we had no such good fortune and we continued on towards Braco. Mais was driving, while such thoughts as I had were probably ranging over distant moors abounding in merlins and hen-harriers, or scouring some loch for a likely family of common scoters. Suddenly I was jerked back to reality. "Hang on. I think that's it. Over there, just beyond the fence." There, no more than a dozen yards away, a pair of red-legged partridges were placidly feeding. It was an abrupt, unlooked-for end to the long, winding trail. We stopped and bid the birds a grateful good evening. Blissfully oblivious to this solemn moment of history, they did not even trouble to look up — or was it mere imagination that detected from one a slow, knowing, partridge wink? We moved on, our thoughts now turning, not strangely, to celebration.

There were still two days to spare; two days for that golden eagle, that pied woodpecker, one of those mythical Gleneagles magpies. But there was not the remotest desire to be greedy. Putting our feet up had rather more to recommend it. For what, after all, is in a mere list?

Sighting

Yesterday
Six geese came back from Iceland
Hobbling over our October floods
Their voices like scrapes from ancient instruments
Complaining, out of tune, cantankerous
Before landing on the runway of their old field
For a huddled debate about grass and snow
As distant relatives and friends
Came in grey arrowheads far behind.

From close beside the Heart Wood: Aberfeldy, Weem Rock and Farragon.

ENJOYING THE WOODS AND THE TREES

The Motorway Forest

So near the slush of traffic
I am left standing here in no-man's land
With never ceasefire.

I go green beneath the branches
And a storm of finches glitter up
Silvering the light. A roe deer
Shod with moss rides through the grass
Healing my own feet
Tarnished by too many roads
Too many stones.
This is a place of forgiveness
Listening for God.

"HEART OF SCOTLAND". The name is given, on the 1:25 000 Ordnance Survey map, to a little green patch of woodland close beside Aberfeldy. It is an imaginative name and the mapmakers have, with a nice touch, drawn in a small area to look vaguely like a heart. Interestingly, it is said that when the wood was planted around 1850, this shape was not intended, and that it was the locals who came up with the idea that it really was the heart of Scotland. However that may be, the claim is certainly made — with a dash of ingenuity — that if diagonals are drawn across the map from Cape Wrath to Gretna and from John o'Groats to the Mull of Galloway, the point at which they intersect is just west of Aberfeldy. The calculation is out by no more than a mere dozen miles or thereabouts, so perhaps the idea is not altogether too fanciful.

Sadly, at the time of writing at least, the Heart Wood is not as attractive as it might be: a plentiful but rather uneven patchwork of birch, with oaks and sycamores straggling along the lower fringe and here and there occasional conifers in splendid isolation; on the bold central plateau wizened spruce stumps thrusting like bristles through the thin skin of turf. The drystane dyke which edges much of the wood is sadly decrepit, with gaps and gashes, some little more than bedraggled ridges of moss.

Admittedly on an early morning visit in spring one may hear there the battering of a greater spotted woodpecker or the strident "see-er, see-er, see-er" of a tree pipit. On the other hand, a summer crossing has little other than views to offer, and descending the north face when the bracken is at its deepest and toughest is suggestive of jungle warfare. How cheering it would be if the pillaged crown of the old wood were to be widely replanted, with further generous native Scots additions to the cluster of two dozen saplings, the beginnings of a recent planting scheme, set in one of the top corners. The whole eminence could be made a real showpiece — Perthshire's heart as well as the heart of Scotland; for surely there is more woodland diversity and interest in Perthshire than in any other county in the length or breadth of the land.

On one of those nondescript afternoons of March when spring is not quite sure if it has arrived or not, I made my way up to the Heart Wood. Occasional soft showers were following each other in from the west, and across on the far side of the valley a drift of mist half hid Farragon and Meall nan Tairneachan, "the hill of the thunderings". It was the kind of day which is particularly enjoyable and not just for the sense of satisfaction at having chosen to forego armchair comfort at the fireside.

I found it disheartening nevertheless to work round the old boundary dyke and imagine what might have been thriving within it on the present empty expanses of grass and rushes. It was more cheering to think by way of contrast of the next part of my afternoon walk: the familiar arrow-straight avenue alongside the former cow park, from Wade's bridge to Weem. I could only hope that, like the imaginative road-edging there, the old Heart Wood would soon be given new life and made to flourish once more.

I dropped down quickly to the bridge. There the daffodil banks were full-budded, almost in flower and not too long beaten in the race by a bright mass of crocuses. The river, wickedly full, was sleek and in a hurry. Over the bridge itself an unexpected, purposeful cormorant planed in to get busy downstream with some early evening fishing.

It is not so long since the majestic avenue of Lombardy poplars, once one of the spectacular wonders of the county, lined the road from Wade's bridge. Unfortunately in 1975 and 1976 the trees, by then almost 80 years old, had to be felled as they were starting to blow down. It was a particularly sad loss for those familiar with this impressive approach to Aberfeldy.

Happily, however, in 1989 and 1990 a re-planting programme was undertaken through the Scottish Community Woods Campaign. Thanks to the remarkable enthusiasm of over 200 volunteers, young and old, nearly 300 aspens were planted along the roadside edges. Most imaginatively a special relationship between town and trees was forged by allowing each individual planter to have his or her ownership recorded — a move so popular that at times there was even queuing to obtain a tree to plant.

Aspens, Scotland's native poplars, were deliberately chosen as replacements for the foreign Lombardy trees. Not so tall but much more bushy, they are especially spectacular in autumn in their vivid shimmering yellow. More suited too to Perthshire wildlife, their leaves are particularly appetising to caterpillars such as the puss moth. Now clear of their protective chrysalis-tubes, the new trees will surely not be long in once again forming an avenue to be proud of.

Not, indeed, that the double row of young aspens will ever grow to rival the world's tallest hedge — at Meikleour, right across near the eastern fringe of the county. Now over 110 feet high, lining each side of the road, the famous old beech hedge was planted in 1746. In those days, apparently, it was the custom to build a dyke as shelter for a new hedge, and it is recorded how on that occasion some of the men engaged on the construction of the wall left to fight in the battle of Culloden. Since those early days the hedge has had to be regularly pruned — indeed if it were not trimmed now every ten years or so, it would soon degenerate and might well have to be felled. At the time of a recent pruning a sophisticated hydraulic platform and five-man team had to be employed, at a cost of some £16,000. Prior to that the work was being carried out by the local fire brigade and teams of steeplejacks.

For my own March afternoon sortie a 45-minute saunter past the aspens and round the forest trail above Weem seemed a fitting conclusion. The Weem Rock path, which climbs steeply enough to St. David's Well, keeps clear for the most part of the unruly sea of rhododendrons drowning so extensively most of the old walkways of the past. Though still raw in places and often muddy low down, it has been sensibly engineered by the Forestry Commission, with staircases here and there and suitably sited guard rails. There is still plenty tangled ground cover round about, and I was given a cheery welcome by a succession of particularly vocal wrens, the decibels they produced far outclassing the mewing of a buzzard half-glimpsed through the trees higher up.

Weem Rock was once a beacon station of Clan Menzies from which the chief was able to summon his followers in times of trouble. How good it would be if the path were to be continued (as indeed has been suggested) in a further succession of zigzags to the old summit lookout point, commanding superb peregrine's eye views up and down Strathtay, and incidentally lending considerably more significance to the trail itself.

Also closely associated with Clan Menzies — if hardly as well known as it deserves to be — is the fine specimen of a strawberry tree which grows a short distance from the north-east corner of the castle. Now some 40 feet tall, it is remarkable for its clusters of white flowers in spring, its orange-red fruit and also for the typical characteristic of its kind — curling outer bark which peels off easily to disclose striking light terra-cotta underbark. The tree brings to mind the little-known story of Archibald Menzies who was the discoverer of the species and after whom it was named.

Archibald Menzies was born in the parish of Weem in 1754, and in due course became a naval ship's surgeon; this enabled him to travel the world and, as a brilliant botanist, to fulfil his consuming passion for plant-collecting. Among the impressive variety of trees and plants with which he enriched our countryside, he was responsible for introducing the sitka spruce into this country from the West Coast of America — perhaps an achievement of questionable merit in some people's eyes today. He was responsible, too, for the introduction to Britain in 1795 of the monkey puzzle tree, having surreptitiously purloined a few of the tree's edible seeds while he was being entertained to dinner by the Viceroy of Chile. It had been three years earlier, in 1792, while exploring the then little-known coast of California with the master of his ship, Captain Vancouver, that he made a whole variety of discoveries of new species, among them "his own" strawberry tree, *Arbutus menziesii*.

Another of Perthshire's individual wonders is the old yew tree in Fortingall churchyard. Our most recent visit to it was on a late afternoon in mid-October, when low autumn mist barely above tree height was bringing early dusk. The evening, I remember, was to darken quickly into a night of much confusion for the geese, plaintive and clamorous, not long arrived from Iceland. The conditions were undoubtedly fitting for taking a look at the ancient tree, with its black gnarled trunk and foliage so dark as to be suggestively funereal. It seemed almost sinister, crouched low in its walled churchyard corner.

Three thousand years old, they say it is; possibly the most ancient piece of vegetation in Europe. A remarkable survivor from the far-off depths of Perthshire's history. Mere centuries ago, of course, yews were particularly highly prized for their value in providing wood for bows. Thomas Pennant, who visited Fortingall

Autumn colour show: the track by the Tay near Dunkeld Cathedral.

on both his Scottish tours, in 1769 and 1772, was prompted to comment: "Our ancestors seem to have had a classical reason for planting these dismal trees among the repositories of the dead, and a political one for placing them near their houses. In the days of archery, so great was the consumption of this species of wood, that the bowyers were obliged to import considerable quantities." Another possible reason, of course, why the trees are found so often in corners of cemeteries and graveyards out of the normal reach of children and animals is that all parts of the yew, except strangely enough for the bright scarlet seed-covering,are exceptionally poisonous.

Two other giants, not indeed as venerable as the Fortingall yew but nevertheless with time-spans remarkable enough to single them out as special, are the magnificent cedar of Lebanon at Moness House, Aberfeldy, and the still more famous Birnam oak, rather less than half a mile down-river from Telford's bridge at Dunkeld.

The cedar is reputed to date from Prince Charlie's day and certainly there is something almost regal about the immaculately straight trunk and long sweeping branches — an excellent excuse for a meal with a view at Moness House Hotel, originally the mansion of the Flemyngs, Barons of Moness, who held land hereabouts for 300 years.

The exact age of the Birnam oak is uncertain, the description on the nearby plinthed tablet being cautiously worded — "several centuries old", giving nothing away. The late Seton Gordon was more daring, describing it as "believed to be over 1,000 years old and to be a relic of the original Birnam wood of the time of Macbeth." Certainly, with its gigantic trunk hollowed with age into a cave, gaping like a decaying molar, and branches so massive that no less than seven of them have to be supported on crutches, the tree looks almost unbelievably ancient. Its near neighbour, a huge sycamore, can be classed as a comparative youngster, its

Past history: the former poplar avenue between Aberfeldy and Weem. (**"The Courier", Dundee.**)

age having been assessed at a mere 300 years or thereabouts.

If the old Birnam oak together with its sycamore neighbour makes no more than a snack, swiftly demolished, a whole satisfying banquet is there for the taking around Dunkeld itself and just beyond, almost immediately up-river. This is Atholl country *par excellence*, a part of the best of Perthshire to be discovered, enjoyed and re-discovered all over again.

It was our friend Jim Chapman who first took me on a Dunkeld woodland roundabout one brilliant morning of late October — a morning to remember for its riotous display of rust and gold and flame. Jim is a forester with a lifetime of experience in various countries of Africa, most recently in Malawi. Now retired, he has been waging from home a non-stop battle for the preservation of the threatened forests round Mount Mulanje, a battle he is very determined to win. Often, no doubt, in his fighting he recalls the survey-journeys which he and his wife Betty used to carry out, safaris as tough and intrepid as they were fascinating to read about for those who received their letters.

There was little suggestion of toughness in our quiet circuit, started soberly enough in the car-park at Dunkeld. But there was to be any amount of enjoyment in our tour; after all this was, Jim commented, "the forester's Mecca". Certainly as we progressed it was a rare pleasure to hear his observations on species after species which in ordinary circumstances, with my deplorably unskilled eye, I would have passed blindly and blithely by: Norway maples and western red cedars; European silver firs, prolific Jim said, in the Jura, the Vosges and the foothills of the Pyrenees; goat willows and least willows, more commonly seen on the slopes of Carn Gorm, up in Glen Lyon; occasional hornbeams, their iron-hard wood ideal for watermill paddles as, for example, on the old millwheel now turning in Aberfeldy. All, in fact, so strange to me that I have no doubt the newly arrived fieldfares, chacking in the leaf canopy overhead, were in fact merely having a good laugh at my ignorance.

In particular, however, it was a day for the viewing of larches. Early on the tour programme was a look at the one remaining "parent larch" at the western edge of the cathedral grounds. Now standing tall at over 100 feet, it

was immensely impressive as we saw it, its huge branches a massive spread of red autumn rust, the deep carpeting round its base a billion matching needles.

The tree's great height and girth make it not too difficult to realise that it is just over 250 years old. Planted in 1738 by the 2nd Duke of Atholl, it was one of five seedlings brought over from the Tyrol by Colonel Menzies, of Glen Lyon — the first larch trees to be grown in the Scottish Highlands. At first the seedlings were treated as greenhouse plants, but as they did not appreciate such coddling, they were thrown out. Fortunately they did well on the refuse dump to which they had been consigned and grew to become the source of seed for the widespread larch plantings carried out by the Dukes of Atholl in the 18th and 19th centuries. Sadly it is only the one great tree which remains of the original quintet, four having been felled for timber.

In passing it is perhaps of interest to note that almost 200 years ago, in the Dunkeld parish report of the old *Statistical Account*, it is mentioned that since the time that larches had been cultivated, crossbills had appeared in the woods; other "rarities" also occasionally being seen were great grey shrikes and green woodpeckers.

From the grand old "parent" tree we made our way along the bank of the Tay — a particularly beautiful walk that bright October morning, the path a lavish scattering of fallen leaves, the river glinting silver, the trees a hundred tints of gold. It would have been good to spin out the pleasure beyond Dunkeld House, but instead we circled back through the hotel grounds to see more larches of interest on Kennel Bank. Here seedlings from the famous parents were planted around 1750, some still standing and distinguished by their splendid tall, straight stems. Nearby, in 1887, eleven imported Japanese larches were also planted, resulting in the hybrid trees now so popular and widespread throughout the country.

The original European trees, Jim told me, later came to be known as "boat skin" larches, so named on account of their use as particularly tough, durable "skins" for fishing boat hulls, mostly on the Scottish east coast. Not, in fact, that this had been any new discovery. Back near the end of the 18th century the writer of the

Dunkeld parish report, once again in the old *Statistical Account*, recorded: "The larix is fit for every purpose almost of the carpenter, is very hardy as a plant, and very lasting when in use. It has been found to resist, much longer than any other wood, the alternations of wet and dry. The Duke of Atholl caused one of the boats at the ferry here to be constructed of the larix wood; and a plank of oak, from a tree 30 years old, was put in for a test of the comparative durability of each. The oak has decayed, and the larix continues sound."

Conifers once again comprised the main focus of attention on another not far distant round little more than a month later. On this occasion my companion was Gunnar Godwin. Now retired apart from part-time consultancy work, Gunnar can look back on a particularly impressive Forestry Commission career in Scotland, England and Wales. A conservator in districts both north and south of the Border, a former president of the Institute of Chartered Foresters and a member of numerous forestry and wildlife trusts and societies, he nevertheless delighted me by showing every sign of complete enjoyment on a very humble trail.

We started in familiar, well-trodden territory just a mile up-river from Dunkeld — on the National Trust for Scotland's woodland walk at the Hermitage. For an early December morning it was more than just amiably mild: the sun shone free and there was not the least hint of frost. Even the Braan, unusually subdued below red-carpeted banks, did not seem to know it was winter.

It was only minutes to the stately company of Douglas firs, standing tall before the old bridge and the folly. These splendid trees seem almost to compete with each other for attention and one can imagine an impartial referee having to be brought along to decide whether any are beating the par figure of 0.61 metres' growth in a year. According to Gunnar, this could be seen in the topmost tips of the firs, but as the tallest of these now reach to heights of between 160 and 170 feet, accurate measurement — to the layman at least — has a chancy look about it.

We paused to look down on the deep, peat-dark pool and the feeder fall which explodes into it from the jagged rock gut under the folly. Gunnar had worked hereabouts in days gone by, so it was good to have a kind of proprietorial

A glimpse of the Hermitage folly through the River Braan woods.

regard for trees and river alike. I noticed with momentary alarm that my companion had a far-away look in his eye as he contemplated a rock which would clearly make an ideal diving platform out-thrust over the pool. However, I need not have worried or hinted that a swim within days of Christmas would scarcely have been wise; he was merely thinking nostalgically of the many good bathes he had enjoyed on summer days of the past.

We conceded only a passing nod to Ossian's Hall, and further denied ourselves the equally questionable pleasure of following the muddy path to Ossian's Cave. Like the Hall, this cheerless burrow, with its boulder walls and uninviting seat sliced from the bare rock, dates from the 18th century and seems to have been designed expressly to demonstrate that the ancient bard was one who clearly liked his discomforts. This pleasantly improbable theory might, perhaps, be said to be borne out by a comparison with the even less hospitable Ossian's Cave, dripping, draughty and vegetatious, its floor tilted at an angle of 45°, high on the sunless north face of Aonach Dubh overlooking Glencoe.

We slanted uphill to the first miles of the main Craigvinean Forest track, gaining height steadily between enclosing walls of conifers. Now and again we heard coal tits and goldcrests calling and once, higher, the sudden hustle when a small flock of siskins took off in alarm. Round a sharper curve a squirrel scuttled hesitantly across the track in front of us.

For the most part there was the expected sitka sameness, so that the occasional breaks with glimpses down to Dunkeld and the sparkle of the Tay were all the more welcome. Variety was lent also by some grey poplars by the trackside early on and shortly afterwards by a whole army of European larch seedlings, just overtopping the thick ground cover of broom and catching the rich gold of the morning sunshine.

One of the places where Gunnar had worked in the past was on Craig-y-Barns, the sheer-faced rock crag on the far side of the valley which was background to most of the views we had past the nearer sitkas. The story of its early afforestation is told by the Rev. Hugh Macmillan in his book *The Highland Tay*:

The way in which the precipitous eminences of Craig-y-Barns and Craig Vinean were clothed with trees, invests them with a wonderful interest. Originally they towered up to heaven bare and gaunt in their hoary nakedness; their sides being too precipitous to admit of being planted in the usual way. But Mr Napier, the famous engineer, while on a visit to the Duke of Atholl, suggested that the cannon in front of his host's residence might be loaded with tin canisters, filled with seeds of pine and spruce and larch, and then fired at the Craigs. This was done, when the canisters, striking the rocks, burst like shells, and dispersed the seeds in the cracks and ledges, where they grew, and in course of time formed the vast billows of forest vegetation which have now submerged the highest points of the scenery.

I asked Gunnar if he found the story at all credible, but he appeared to treat my question with a certain amount of contempt. No doubt Forestry Commission methods had progressed significantly by the time he came to be busied with planting.

Today, with its five million trees and complicated jigsaw of tracks and rides, Craigvinean Forest covers a vast spread of hillside, particularly impressive when viewed from lower levels by the Tay. Its highest point is at almost 1700 feet, close to the open moorland which lies beyond the northern edging, so that it offers an invitation hard to resist. My companion certainly looked sufficiently full of energy to make light of the further climb and miles necessary to take us to the top, but after a steady pull up to perhaps half height, enough seemed to me to be enough. We dropped down therefore through a section of broken woodland where felling was in progress to a lower track leading eventually to the main Perth-Inverness road and so back to the Hermitage car-park.

Some parts of the forest which we passed on our way down were of particular interest to Gunnar, as he was able to remember them clearly from years gone by, when their make-up — considerably more of a mixture — was much different from today's. His graphic stories of working trials and tribulations, not just in Perthshire but in other woodlands too — for example on the West Coast where battle had constantly to be joined with rain and midges — made entertaining telling. Perhaps, had we continued our climb to the forest summit, my going might not have been so leaden-footed after all.

It was a day of perfection at the tail-end of August which provided another walk to remember for Mais and me, on this occasion far enough from Dunkeld — through the Black Wood of Rannoch. In the mid-morning heat Loch Rannoch itself lay silk-smooth, and no more than two or three vague shreds of cirrus trailed Everest-high in the powder-blue haze of the sky. The road past Rannoch School was a continuous dappling of shadow and sun, ending for us at the lay-by opposite Blackwood Cottage. High in the roadside pines, heard but not seen, some long-tailed tits gave us greeting as we left the car, their whispered "si-si-si" exchanges speeding us cheerfully on our way.

It was cool among the first of the trees. The path, ideally fashioned, looked inviting — mostly grassy, now and again rusty with a million million pine needles carpeting ancient roots. *Slios garbh*, "the rough slope", they call this south side of Loch Rannoch, but from the start the track's gentle climbing was certainly nothing other than kindly. We paused often, too, to listen to our companion and guide, our friend Tavish Macmillan, formerly Chief Forester in Rannoch, then District Forester for Perthshire, experienced over many busy years and, as bonus addition to that, a first-rate historian. His companion in turn was Sam the spaniel, model of excellent behaviour.

Strikingly dense ground cover crowded to the edges of the path: thickly matted sphagnum moss, ragged purple banks of heather, fat-berried blaeberry plants, more often than not a thigh-deep sea of bracken. Here and there, however, there were brave clusters of pine seedlings a foot or so high, some — as Tavish pointed out — bushy and distorted, due mainly

An August walk in the Black Wood of Rannoch.

to the grazing of red deer, others nevertheless with tall, straight leaders, clearly with every chance of strong, progressive growth. Other trackside trees more immediately obvious were the usual companions of pines — birch, rowan and some goat willow.

And always in the background the magnificent old pines themselves.

"Those two over there," commented Tavish, indicating a particularly spectacular pair, "would be 200 to 250 years old, maybe more. Amusing to think they could well have been there in Prince Charlie's day." And he went on to describe how, long before the Forty-Five, when the Black Wood belonged to the Struan Robertsons, timber had been extracted by the "loggers" and floated on Loch Rannoch to the Tummel, the Tay and the sea; how pines had been sold to provide the "cooms" necessary for the building of Wade's bridge at Aberfeldy (then used

One of the old Scots pines near Camghouran.

again later in the roof of Amulree church); how after the Rising, administration of the woodlands by the Commissioners of the Forfeited Estates had brought much improvement, as also, to some extent, had management last century by the Wentworth family. When the West Highland Railway was being constructed, many trees were felled for use as railway sleepers; in the First World War the Wood was marked out for use and was saved from total destruction only by the Armistice; in the Second, felling took toll of a large proportion of the Wood.

It was shady and cool on the path, and thanks to Tavish's entertaining commentary we scarcely noticed the gradient. In the old wood quietness and peace are there for the taking,

and it was no surprise near the highest point to glimpse a wide open space where once a croft is said to have stood — "Robertson's clearing". Surely a man of contentment, that Robertson; for how indeed could he be other in that remote, rarely frequented sanctuary not far from the Black Wood's western fringe?

At this point, on the other side of our path, a section of the wood had been fenced in — an experiment, we were told, started not long after the Forestry Commission took over in 1947. The idea was to allow the natural regeneration of the area complete freedom of growth unhindered by grazing and undisturbed by either felling or sowing. Results had been remarkable: outside the fence a fairly sparse scattering of trees in the usual thick mat of ground cover; inside a massed shoulder-to-shoulder crowd of youngish trees, almost all birch and rowan; the pines apparently would be following on at their own more sedate pace.

The walk was level now, then gently downhill. Now and again we had window glimpses of Loch Rannoch and, beyond, of the heather slopes topping the Talla Bheith woodland. At our feet scabious and harebells, sinister-looking ochreous toadstools, an anthill scurryingly alive. Once we paused to measure two impressive pines in mid-path — each was 3½ inches tall. (We wondered how they may look in A.D. 2200). I was disappointed that, as it was the wrong time of year, we would see no green hairstreak butterflies, said to be regular inhabitants of the wood. Everywhere, always, the beautiful, reddish glow of branches and bark of the magnificent, gnarled old pines.

For the final quarter mile we dropped down a corridor of path more darkly overgrown. Here the prolific growth of birch and rowan close set on either hand seemed to stress afresh the essential variety of the walk — with the lochside stretch back to the car a round of no more than 2½ miles. We sat down by the shore, appropriately perhaps on the bleached white tentacles of an ancient pine stump. In the sunsparkle out on the loch an occasional fish managed a half-hearted jump. The far background hills near the foot of Loch Ericht showed hazily withdrawn in the heat. What more was there to have asked for?

In the course of its long and chequered history the Black Wood seems to have come closest to obliteration in the early years of last century. Writing in 1883 in his book *Woods, Forests and Estates of Perthshire*, Thomas Hunter told how the formidable snags and setbacks met with in attempts to float the trees to the Tay and the sea made the work so financially prohibitive that they were in fact hidden blessings which resulted in the saving of the old Wood.

We have mentioned that the area of the Black Wood is not at present so extensive as it was during last century. This is greatly to be regretted, but it is matter for profound satisfaction that the famous wood was not completely obliterated, as at one time was being rapidly accomplished by contract. About the beginning of the present century, a portion of the wood was sold to a Public Company belonging to the south, who felled a great part of it, and would have carried off considerably more timber, but for the lucky circumstance, at least for the country, that the enterprise failed to prove remunerative owing to the difficulty of transit, etc. Although the Company did not prosper, it was the means of doing some little good to the district while the operations lasted. At that time the country was in a very bad state, bordering almost on famine. Meal could scarcely be procured at any price, work was scarce, and labourers only too plentiful. The cutting down of the Black Wood was, accordingly, looked upon at the time as a providential circumstance, and proved a great blessing to many of the poor people in the district, as the Company imported provisions from the south to supply the workers in a way that was impossible for the natives to do without extraneous aid. Indeed, so great was the poverty at this time, and the scarcity of oatmeal — the staple food of the people of this and other parts of Scotland — that no more than one half boll of meal was distributed at a time to a single family, the rest of their supplies having to be made up with sea biscuits.

History for the Black Wood has certainly never stood still. The backward glimpses we have of it, as the mists of the centuries part and close and part again, are striking. And now, with heightened appreciation of the forest's unique ecological value, it has had the spotlight turned fairly and squarely on its future. Meetings in 1975 between the Forestry Commission and the Nature Conservancy Council looked closely at the all-important question of regeneration — with the cruel felling of the past, the dense ground cover of old heather and deep mosses, and the appetite of the deer (resident roe, more occasional red) all in their own ways hostile. It was agreed to declare the Wood a forest nature reserve under the continued management of the Commission, not in order to maintain it in its present depleted state, but to achieve in the long term what "it may perhaps have been in the 15th century before large-scale exploitation began." An exciting ideal, a tremendous promise; a rich promise to span the years, the decades, even the centuries to come.

From Rannoch's *slios garbh* of the 21st century it is good to swing the spotlight round again to focus — seemingly rather oddly — on an unobtrusive shop window in Aberfeldy. Here, on show behind the glass, headlined newspaper cuttings and a bright surround of photographs have been boldly blazoning displays such as "Growing up with Trees" and "Keep Growing Native Trees" — variations on another lively far-seeing theme.

The story they tell may be said to go back to June 1982 and the inspiration of dedicated conservationist Alan Drever, at that time countryside ranger in Aden Country Park, near Peterhead. Putting into practice his idea of establishing mini native tree nurseries in school grounds, he involved local schoolchildren in literally living with their own trees, from the fun of seed collection to actual planting out four years later. Not only is this a thoroughly popular learning exercise for the youngsters, but it can be of remarkable practical value also: for example, a single nursery as small as three square metres in area can produce as many as 400 trees for planting out each year.

From this experimental beginning great things have grown. In 1988 the Scottish Community Woods Campaign was launched. Now known as Scottish Native Woods and based in Aberfeldy, it is the only national organisation dealing strictly with the conservation of our tiny fragile remnant of native woodlands — our oak and birch, our rowan and hazel and holly, and in the Highlands, of course, our Caledonian pine. With strong emphasis on native trees, landowners are being encouraged to concentrate on this particular aspect of management. As additional incentive, vigorous research into new markets for hardwoods is being carried out. Thus, alongside the thriving children's "Growing up with Trees" campaign, the whole thing could well be described as a steadily growing rescue operation. More in fact than that; much more: it is a contribution of immense importance to the whole exciting continuation of the Perthshire woodlands story.

The Chestnut Days

I breathe again the chestnut-fallen stillness after storm
Have all those years been buried by the snow
Each shuffling shade of autumns past
Since I, blown through the horse-galloping grass
Found tawny lions curled in shining state.

WADE ROAD

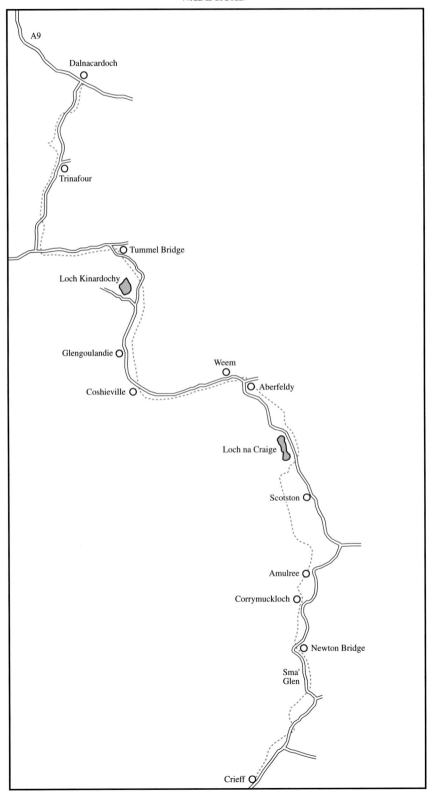

ENJOYING A WADE ROAD

Wayside Encounter — Highland Bull

He is just an ornament on the moorland
Made of heather roots, too tough for meat
A piece of old machinery with handlebars
Left out to rust in all weathers.

Americans will stop their cars
In a force ten August, iron rain —
Looking for the bull's front end
And a snatched picture.

Yet in him somewhere is an engine room
Quite capable of firing.
Tickle the bracken beast
With care, with a little Gaelic.

"BRIGHT PERIODS and showers, some heavy and with hail." So ran the forecast for the day at the tail-end of March. An interesting outlook, I decided. And, thinking ahead to the various stages of the walk I had planned, I could not help wondering if it was not more than just the weather that promised to be a thoroughly odd mixture.

The plan I had in mind was to follow General Wade's old military road all the way from Crieff to Dalnacardoch, the point at which it merges with the present A9. As the total distance of this worked out at almost 50 miles, it would clearly be necessary to divide it into several sections — preferably not too strenuous and arranged so as to span an enjoyable number of weeks. I hoped the General himself would have thought it a good idea.

Pleasingly enough, my starting-point in Crieff had a real personal touch to it: it was beside the old well in a former garden of ours — more accurately the half well, since it was shared with our next-door neighbours. This must obviously have been an excellent stopping-place in the old days, as it lay only some 25 yards from Wade's introductory stretch (now Ferntower Road) climbing steadily uphill, typically arrow-straight, from the centre of Crieff. We used often to imagine Wade's men, even perhaps with the General himself looking on, having a well-earned tea-break by the side of the well, during some particularly back-breaking spell with pick and shovel.

It was in 1730 that Wade had been allowed a Treasury grant for his "new road for wheel carriages" to run from Crieff to Dalnacardoch. Before that, presumably, the route would have been well trodden by countless drovers and their cattle-beasts, but meriting nevertheless the pithy general summing-up of Edward Burt, Wade's agent and surveyor, in his *Letters from a Gentleman in the North of Scotland*:

The Highlands are but little known even to the Inhabitants of the low Country of Scotland, for they have ever dreaded the Difficulties and Dangers of Travelling among the Mountains; and when some extraordinary Occasion has obliged any one of them to such a Progress, he has, generally speaking, made his Testament before he set out, as though he were entering upon a long and dangerous Sea Voyage, wherein it was very doubtful if he should ever return.

No doubt the new road would have come quickly and thankfully into use, and by the time the Jacobite troops marched up it on their way northwards before Culloden, it would have become a well-known, well-used highway.

The General Wade portrait on the wall of Weem Inn.

Prince Charlie and his army were certainly in my mind's eye that March morning as I reached the top of Crieff golf course and looked down on the wide expanse below ruined Ferntower House, where on that day two and a half centuries ago the Prince had reviewed his troops. The gusting west wind was at my back as I turned and continued along the muddy track round the Knock — or Cnoc as the Gaelic would have it, meaning "hillock" or "knoll". Among the trees it was sheltered, and the added warmth of one of the morning sun-blinks made me think of the accompaniment of bird-song there would be there in only a few weeks' time — willow-warblers in abundance, garden warblers here and there, possibly even one of the none-too-numerous Crieff chiffchaffs. Yet that morning, too, I had kindly welcome enough, with chaffinch and wren, robin and great tit vigorously in competition. Once a squirrel scampered closely across my path, mocking my weighty tread with its agility.

Opposite the entrance to the grounds of Monzie Castle, the obvious, tree-bordered furrow of the Wade road slanted pleasantly uphill to the main A822, and now the view westwards was beginning to open out — to the vague snow-wreaths on Ben Voirlich and Stuc a'Chroin, bleakly shawled in mist. Fortunately the main road section was brief, the Wade line breaking away at a prominent larch, to run straight once more across a spongy mile of moorland. Here curlews and peewits and the first larks I had heard kept trying to persuade me that spring had really come. Somehow I could not help recalling that the last time I had been on that particular stretch of moor a friend and I had been caught in a raging snow-blizzard and we had stumbled into the sanctuary of Foulford Inn feeling like a couple of antarctic explorers back from a march to the Pole.

From Foulford over the intervening hillside and down into the Sma' Glen beyond is as delightful a section as any of Wade's old road. A climb of some 250 feet, with, midway, a small, renovated bridge over the Fendoch Burn, leads to open heather moorland. Here snow-patches lay in the hollows, and as if the latter were not enough to remind me that winter was still not quite past, a heavy sleet shower came sweeping in to attack. Grey-white curtains drifted on the wind across the slopes ahead, blotting out any views of the higher ridges above the Sma' Glen itself. I was soon wet and chilled, so that it was a pleasant relief to drop down at last to the main road and, half a mile further on, huddle in shelter behind a thin screen of larches. Ten minutes later the car arrived to pick me up and take me home in sodden discomfort to Aberfeldy.

A fortnight later my wife and I took up where I had left off, midway through the Sma' Glen. We were dropped by friends bound for Crieff, our own car having been left five miles back at Amulree. The time was 5 p.m.

In his usual shrewdly observant manner Edward Burt gives a brief but graphic description of the Sma' Glen — "a Hollow so very narrow, and the Mountains on each Side so steep and high, that the Sun is seen therein no more than between two and three Hours in the longest Day." The quotation was certainly apt for us that April afternoon, with the glen already deep in shadow and the wind tugging at us with a touch that was doubly icy after the pleasant warmth of the car. As we set off across the flats beside the River Almond, I could not help thinking of the ring-ouzels due back about then from their winter quarters in the mountains of Tunisia or the High Atlas of Morocco. Hopefully the weather would manage a hint of Mediterranean warmth to inspire their piping up among the hillside rocks above where we were, or higher up Glen Almond beyond Newton Bridge.

In rather less than half a mile we were at Clach Ossian, the massive seven-foot high boulder which Wade's men, with mighty effort, had to move out of the way. Again according to Burt, "The Soldiers, by vast Labour, with their Levers and Jacks, or Hand-screws, tumbled it over and over, till they got it quite out of the Way, although it was of such an enormous Size that it might be Matter of great Wonder how it could ever be removed by Human Strength and Art, especially to such as had never seen an Operation of that Kind." One cannot help suspecting that Wade and his soldiers rather enjoyed the challenge of moving the big boulder in order not to spoil the straightness of the road; a modest deviation to skirt round it would surely not have been too difficult.

A short distance above Newton Bridge, which we reached in an easy half hour, the old road swings left over the Lurg Burn, here dropping steeply down to join the Almond. The simple little grass-topped bridge is such a perfect example of Wade's artistry at its best, that it is always difficult not to stop to take a photograph or two. This occasion was no different, and my only regret was that there was no chance to recapture the past in a dramatic pageant of colour with a detachment of Highlanders or redcoats marching bravely across to the skirl of pipes or echoing fifes and drums.

On the open moor beyond there was no shelter from the bitter east wind, although we were back in sunshine once more. This next stage, to Corrymuckloch farm, was exactly two miles, first very obviously over rough, boggy heather, then mostly by way of the main road between familiar stretches of grassland. Out on the heather there were no birds, not even a grouse, so it was a real pleasure on the last quarter-mile to be welcomed by curlews, joyously tumbling peewits and a strident pair of redshanks. The splendid herd of highland cattle, so often to be seen at the roadside near Corrymuckloch and surely the most photographed beasts in Scotland, was this evening a mere cluster of

The inscription on the parapet of Wade's bridge, Aberfeldy.

rusty dots on a relatively distant hillside. In our family we know them affectionately as "the woolly bullies"; it was a disappointment not to be greeting them at closer quarters.

Only a mile and a half remained to Amulree — straight as a die the whole way from the edge of the farm territory at Corrymuckloch. It made an ideal climax to our walk, with an incidental glimpse of a whole company of hares, half-changed from their conspicuous winter white, and long views over the foreground ochre and Vandyke brown of the moor to Loch Freuchie and the vague snow-smudges on the Carn Mairg group of hills at the entrance to Glen Lyon.

And so, pleasantly tired, to Amulree Hotel.

How incalculably often, down the years, must Amulree have been an immensely welcome stopping-point! For the drovers, nearing journey's end at Crieff tryst after the long, slow miles southward with their beasts, or starting off homewards once more, silver and gold crying out to be squandered, with rollicking good cheer at the inn. Later — after Wade's day — as an official King's House set beside the King's highway, it was to accommodate Prince Charlie for a night on his march north to tragedy. And for Wade himself it would certainly have been a thoroughly familiar halting-place. The Braan, only a stone's throw further on, is a sizeable little river and must have given the General and his "highwaymen", as he affectionately called his men, no little cause for concern. Often enough during their building of the bridge they would be thankful for refreshment at the old inn, and one can well imagine the "top brass", right convivially minded, clumping in at some long day's end for dinner, bed and breakfast. By comparison, our own bar supper may have been suitably modest, but perhaps not so very much less enjoyed.

In several ways the first third of the next section was the most enjoyable of the entire walk to Dalnacardoch. For one thing it took us right away from the main road, so far indeed that the latter quite simply might not have existed at all. For another, most of it was typical "Wade" — a furrow some twelve feet wide between banks and marker boulders, mostly running immaculately straight, and with a central carpet of springy turf delightful to tread. Most satisfying of all perhaps, when one did come over a rise or round one of the rare bends, there was the road

Typical "Wade": where his road crosses the Lurg Burn near Newton Bridge, Glen Almond.

stretching ahead, beckoning forward to new settings and new outlooks — always a little further.

It was now well on in April, and three of us — my wife, our friend Andrew McNab, from Crieff, and myself — had left the first of the two cars we were using parked by the roadside a mile on the Aberfeldy side of Scotston farm; the second had brought us to Amulree. The afternoon was a pleasant one of sunshine, with towering cumulus clouds and only a few distant scowls of hail-showers. On the horizon hills the patches of snow seemed almost to be shrinking visibly with the promise of new warmth to come. Beside us as we walked, the plaintive exchanges of the blackfaces and their lambs, the shrilling of lark after climbing lark and the ecstasies of the steep-swooping peewits all joined to chorus the joyous magnificat of spring.

The Fender Burn in its deep-set hollow — reached all too soon after that particularly enjoyable first mile — must have called originally for a substantial bridge; now there is nothing, only jagged edges, abrupt as the gap left by

a newly drawn tooth. Hard toil must certainly have been needed: not gunpowder blasting perhaps, but tough, back-breaking navvying none the less. One can almost hear the clank and clatter of the spades and crowbars, the heavier thud of pickaxe and sledgehammer. It is only a pity that there is not a video available today showing the redcoats, hot and dust-grimed and sweating, clustered purposefully beside the slowly narrowing gap. The burn itself as we found it was easily crossed, but it was not difficult to guess at the awkward hazard it would have presented at a time of violent, pounding spate.

Up the slope beyond there was a short, more stony climb, then a deceptive right turn followed by a swing back along forestry edges. Thereafter a gentle descent took us down to the main road once again. Two supremely enjoyable miles were behind us — cause enough for celebration with a five-minute rest, some lemon tea and a biscuit.

The remainder of the day's quota lay across open moorland — a line that started beyond the

One of the miniature bridges on the Wade road opposite Scotston.

A826 near the Cochill Burn, then re-crossed the road to begin a two-mile stretch through the heather, ruler straight apart from a kink or two round the intrusive flanks of a burn. The going varied from squelchy patches of marsh to pleasantly dry surfaces of what looked like Wade's original fine gravel. Some of these latter sections would be easily motorable, and one can readily imagine the General travelling over them in the heavy coach which he used when out on surveys and which seems to have been a source of amazement to the local Highlanders. No doubt we were better off on foot, with the cheery accompaniment of numerous larks and an occasional curlew. We had excellent views, too, of a herd of some 70 red deer straggling across the road ahead. Then we were dropping down over an exasperating stretch of holes and hummocks to another loop of the Cochill. Here, keenly looked forward to, were the two Wade miniatures — Disneyland bridges so small as to be almost laughable, yet built with typical artistry and care. They are real little masterpieces well worth seeing — before they are buried for good beneath a sad shroud of sitkas. Soon they will be lost except to the few who know of their existence and will take the trouble to visit them in the dark depths of the new plantings.

The mile-long stretch from the bridges to the south end of Loch na Craige is not particularly inspiring; it is indistinct, rough, damp, and cut by a number of awkward ditches. Fortunately the weather made up for any irritations that might have been allowed to spoil our walk along it. The breeze had a pleasant touch of warmth, and bright periods were almost continuous. Our first sandpipers of the season, chasing plaintively round the bends of the Cochill, provided another hint of coming summer, while a dipper, a curlew or two and innumerable meadow pipits added their own touches to the enjoyment. We kept hoping for even a distant glimpse of a short-eared owl, usual enough thereabouts, but we had no luck. I could not help wondering if the owls were less in evidence because even the voles were deciding that they disliked the conifer epidemic as much as we did and had taken their departure in consequence.

For part of the way we had difficulty in deciding what was the exact line of the old road, although following true Wade tradition, we per-

severed as straight as we could through the humps and bumps and tussocks. Then the route became more obvious, an un-typical corkscrew climbing gently right-handed between marker-stones till we were back once more alongside the A826.

It was early May — May of the same unpredictable weather — when I had the chance to complete the first half of the journey, downhill into Aberfeldy. There had been day after day of inky clouds, boisterous blatters of rain and sun-blink intervals that painted innumerable rainbows; few spells, in fact, to cheer the ever-greedy bird-watcher. Yet fortune smiled benignly for me as I started off again beside Loch na Craige: almost unbroken sunshine and a good stiff breeze to nudge me on my way.

At this point Wade and his men had not followed the side of the loch very closely — a trap I had somehow not anticipated — and I had another brief skirmish with puddles and plantings before I hit the true line, a delightful three-quarter-mile straight stretch running a hundred yards from the loch. Thoughtfully, today's foresters have left the heathery trough of the old road unplanted, and although in due time it will doubtless be no more than a tunnel between the dark spruces, for the present at least it is sheer pleasure. Here and there rain-pools mirrored blue of sky and white of clouds; then my gaze was drawn farther afield as the Tay valley opened up — first Farragon, then Schiehallion with its speckling of snow-patches, then the whole horizon of the hills from Carn Mairg to the four tops of Beinn a'Ghlo.

Below the roadside viewpoint I managed to tangle myself briefly in another frustration of ditches and infant trees; then, as if to laugh at my stupidity, the familiar Wade furrow suddenly reappeared and led me pleasantly down to the close-cropped grass and barking dogs of Gatehouse. From then on it was familiar home territory, through the first scattering of birches and down past the old Pitilie curling-pond, hidden away among its damp invading trees. Now forgotten and melancholy, the pond has little about it to recall the matches of almost a century ago when it first came into use: the excitement, the shouts, the jollification. But that was all long after Wade; the jollification in his day would happen another quarter mile down the road, at the old inn of Tigh na Leacain, "the house on the face of the brae".

It is now the Old Crieff Road which continues down to the Square in Aberfeldy. Formerly known as the Tomchulan Road, after an old thatched cottage of that name, it crosses the minute Tomchulan Burn, famous for the 8lb salmon taken from it by a small boy one autumn day of phenomenal spate many years ago. It is good to live, as we do now, within sound of the burn's song when it is high, our house once again on a Wade road just like that other all those miles back at the start of our walk in Crieff.

And so to Wade's "masterpiece" spanning the Tay — built to provide "the only passage over that wild and dangerous river". The old bridge nowadays is taken more or less for granted. Yet before 1733, when it was constructed, things would have been very different. The river must have been a major obstacle — often a decidedly fearsome one — and at times the ferrymen must have been kept remarkably hard at it. Especially this would be so whenever the cattle droves were heading south to the great Crieff and Falkirk trysts, even although the beasts themselves would customarily have to swim. As the Aberfeldy burgh motto puts it: "'S dluth tric bat Abairpheallaidh" — "Swift and often goes the boat of Aberfeldy." Not surprisingly the boatmen seem to have known they were on to a good thing and profited accordingly, for when his bridge was completed Wade is reported to have said that he had fulfilled his intention of "setting the rapacious ferryman and his boats on dry land."

Work on the bridge was started on 23rd April 1733, and, astonishingly, was finished before the year was out. Wade later reported that he had employed "master masons and carpenters sent from ye northern countys of England, who were accustomed to works of that nature. These with some of ye best masons of ye country and about 200 artificers and labourers from ye army were employed for a whole year, the winter season for preparing materials and ye summer in laying ye foundation and in building ye bridge."

Among the soldiers — who were drawn from Scottish regiments — there may well have been keen competition to be detailed for work on the bridge: privates were paid sixpence extra for each day's shift, sergeants a shilling and officers half-a-crown.

Wade claimed to have employed "the best architect in Scotland", the celebrated William Adam, but it is more than likely that the latter was responsible only for fixing the parapet details and the "embellishments", so pleasing to visitors today (and no doubt to Wade himself), if, perhaps, rather less impressive to experts in bridge architecture, while the actual structural design would have been carried out by a senior engineer officer.

It was to be a dozen years before the bridge was given the severe test of strength which it is said Wade regularly had in mind during con-

Once a problem for Wade's "highwaymen": Clach Ossian in the Sma' Glen.

struction work. First, Sir John Cope with his troops and artillery train passed through Aberfeldy and camped in the spacious cow-park on the north side of the river; the next year it was the turn of both Prince Charlie and the Duke of Cumberland, the Prince staying for two nights at Castle Menzies and being followed across the Tay a mere four days later by a contingent of Cumberland's pursuing redcoats. Early in the following century Thomas Telford had some thoroughly uncomplimentary things to say about the old bridge, as reported by his companion, the poet Southey: "At a distance it looks well, but makes a wretched appearance upon close inspection. There are four unmeaning obelisks upon the central arch, and the parapet is so high that you cannot see over it. The foundations also are very insecure, for we went into the bed of the river and examined them." It is amusing to speculate on what their comments might be two and a half centuries later, if they could watch today's cars and monster lorries passing the traffic lights and climbing up and over the old humpback.

An early July morning saw Mais and myself, complete with our cycles, pausing briefly on the crown of the bridge. It was not actually raining, but it was grey and cold, with wisps of mist drifting across the upper slopes of the hills. Off one of the shingle-spits edging the river a pair of mergansers were floating contentedly, untroubled by the tug of the current. From the bank behind them a dipper took off and headed purposefully upstream.

We were, in fact, feeling slightly guilty. The reason for this was quite simply that we had decided to do some cheating — by cycling a few Wade miles instead of walking. The first part of the old road on the north side of the Tay followed much the same line as today's B846. The only minor variation was in Wade's choice of start — a typical bee-line across the flat farmland immediately beyond his bridge to join up with the line of the present main road some 200 yards west of Weem Inn. Thereafter it was much the same as what we knew intimately from scores of past car journeys. To have trailed along it on foot would, we felt, have been largely a waste of time.

A Highland "woolly bully" encountered while following the old Wade road.

Once over the bridge we were soon pedalling happily along the familiar straight and round the curve to the inn. Here we nodded a genial morning greeting to the General, looking down at us from his portrait up on the outside wall. It was at the hostelry in 1733 that he had had his local headquarters, and we wondered idly how he had fared for comfort during his stay, occupying what is the oldest part of the building, dating back, it is said, to 1527. Like the inn at Amulree, Weem was later to become an official King's House, so even in Wade's day it was certainly of considerable importance and would see much coming and going and a deal of conviviality as the new road progressed.

Wade's "mark" is very obvious in the long straight stretches which follow after Weem, past Castle Menzies and on to Coshieville, the only minor obstacle to suggest any trouble at all being the Camserney Burn, and as we saw it, parched as a desert wadi, it did not look in the least hostile. We made unbelievably slow time, my excuse being that the back wheel of my cycle was loose and acting as a particularly irritating brake. However, the prospect of second breakfast spurred us on to Coshieville, where we lost no time in turning round and setting about pedalling back home to Aberfeldy.

From Coshieville Hotel the road winds uphill all the way almost to Glengoulandie deer farm. On foot it took me exactly an hour. It is not perhaps a rewarding stretch for the dyed-in-the-wool Wade enthusiast, but a thoroughly enjoyable walk none the less. Certainly I got the true feel of the Keltney Burn gorge, a scar the best part of two miles long, deep, dark, forbidding, and almost completely unsuspected by the passing motorist. Down in its depths the fine Falls of Keltney are largely hidden by the trees which crowd thickly to the river-verges, and are obviously best seen in winter or early spring. My own feeling as I kept pausing on my way, was that a traverse of the whole length of the gorge would be a splendid expedition, not perhaps in the category of the famous Black Rock of Novar in Easter Ross, but doubtless with its own testing pattern of problems. It was hardly a surprise that when a car crashed off the road to the bottom of the gorge not long after my visit, the passengers, who miraculously escaped injury, had to be airlifted from the depths by helicopter.

There were few traces of Wade. I looked carefully wherever the road crossed burns tumbling into the gorge, but concrete and culverts had done their work of concealment too well. It was to be presumed that the mattress and assortment of rusting cans collected below one passing-place at least had not been jettisoned by redcoats two and a half centuries ago.

Mist had been touching the cone of Schiehallion when I had seen it first from near Coshieville, but now as I approached Glengoulandie, the upper slopes were clear and sun-dappled. There were many deer out on the brae above the farm, and the sight of them put me in mind of the occasion when I had first visited Glengoulandie, in the early summer of 1971. I learned then how the deer park idea had originated with the farmer Mr Harry McAdam, and in a magazine article which I wrote shortly afterwards, I gave the story as he told it to me then: "I suppose," he said, "that it all started with the pet deer we had five or six years ago. We'd picked her up on the hill and reared her, so she was really tame. In fact, things got so out of hand that if you left the door open she'd come into the house and make a meal of the curtains. Sometimes she'd even pull the supper cloth on to the floor and lick up all the sugar. We used to get as many as 30 cars at a time stopping outside on the road just to have a look at this one deer."

Mr McAdam went on to tell me how one summer the hind had disappeared, then turned up again with a stag calf. The pair stayed on for another year or so, then suddenly they vanished, this time for good. However, the idea had been born, and at Christmas, 1969, the McAdams bought a three-year-old stag and three hinds from the Duke of Bedford's herd at Woburn. Later a second stag was added, from the world-famous park-fed herd at Warnham. A promising start had been made, a start which has led to the magnificent herd of today and immense pleasure given to hundreds of summer-time visitors to Perthshire.

Beyond Glengoulandie the road continues to climb, though less aggressively, and I was glad to reach the more level stretch above Loch Kinardochy — sadly, untenanted by any birds — beyond the turn-off to Kinloch Rannoch. All the while I had been persisting in looking out for signs of Wade, but saw none in the least convincing, and came to the conclusion that his line was still being followed more or less exactly by the various later road-makers.

A sandwich at the foot of one of the roadside birches provided a thoroughly welcome break. Not far away a robin gave me greeting and somewhere overhead a buzzard was mewing. Greying up in the west above the wide trough of Loch Rannoch, a cloud army was massing, its threat already noticeable in the damp touch of the breeze. Here surely, over the watershed now and with only downhill work to the Tummel, Wade and his men must have had the occasional satisfied break. They had nevertheless at least two awkward burns — deep-set arms of the Allt Kynachan — still to cross, and some tough engineering must have been needed. Then came a neat little piece of corner-cutting, a typical Wade furrow, straight-driven through the heather.

It was hereabouts that Mais and the car caught me up, tempting me with a lift for the last mile of the day, to Tummel Bridge. It was too easy to fall. After all, the well-worn adage is only too true that "Power corrupts, and horse-power corrupts absolutely."

It was not so very far now to journey's end. Two five-mile stages only: one from Tummel Bridge to Trinafour; the last up the steep hill beyond and down to the A9 at Dalnacardoch.

Autumn had come. Patches and streaks of snow added now to the make-up of the high-ground brindling. But Mais and I were interested more in the riot of colour close at hand than in the upper slopes of Schiehallion and Beinn a' Chuallaich, where mists were curling on the mild west wind. Beauty, we could see, was going to defy description.

Our walk started with a dutiful crossing of the old Wade arch over the Tummel, satisfying in line if inevitably too much patched and pointed to allow it its full two and a half centuries' authenticity. The river was still low after the recent Indian summer, but the brown of its trout-pools seemed wholly in keeping with the infinitely varied colour-range round about. Soon we were at the little hump-back over the Allt Mor, beyond which the road continues near the Tummel for half a mile, then swings right-handed into a long uphill climb. It was here beyond the fork that the colours were at their best: lemon and orange, copper and flame; the gold of the birches a miser's hoard spread over the russet carpet expanse of dead bracken and

tawny "lion grass"; here and there the scarlet of rowans or the cinnamon of larches standing out boldly against the background of bottle-green pines. The road itself, pleasant with the scent of bog myrtle, climbed between twin yellow ribbons of a million fallen birch leaves.

Then the mile-long, slightly up-tilted straight looking out over the moors towards Schiehallion — surely a stretch which must have delighted Wade with its directness and lack of intrusive burns. Perhaps with a lift to their morale, the soldiers here exceeded the normal average expected of each: one and a half yards a day. One can readily imagine pickaxes and shovels being plied more enthusiastically, with foundations easily dug and the usual trench prepared for the stones and smaller gravel surfacing. Here and there sizeable boulders still edge the road, although there seem to have been few "monsters" to cause real trouble. Without any doubt this section and the pleasant half-mile dip down to Trinafour must have come as a thoroughly welcome respite before the much tougher work lying immediately ahead.

In some ways the final stage of the walk, the climax, was the most enjoyable day of all. Not indeed that the weather was all it might have been — a hint of rain on the mild, north-west wind and, as we came out on to the moors above Loch Errochty, low cloud hiding the plateau tops of Drumochter. Yet it *was* the climax, the completion of a plan which had given us many hours of pleasure. And in the day itself there were ingredients enough to ensure that it would be long remembered.

With only one car involved, Mais and I had to do the walk in both directions, altogether the best part of ten miles and up and over some 1200 fairly steep feet. We parked near the rickety, grass-topped old Wade bridge at Trinafour — difficult to view satisfactorily where it spans a secluded rock-corner of the Errochty Water — and set off uphill after a first sitting of lunch. In places alongside the road the usual marker stones stood out prominently, and higher, where the gradient steepened, there were two very obvious traverses. These fierce hairpin bends, set on the steep face of the hill, must have presented the armies of Jacobite days with not a few problems for any equipment and supplies that needed much manhandling. Even if the heavy ordnance and baggage trains were brought more easily north by way of Dunkeld and Killiecrankie, there must still, one imagines, have often been a deal of toil and sweat demanded by this tough gradient above Trinafour.

The upper moors, so vibrant in summer with the music of the larks and curlews and now and again the piping of golden plovers, were deserted and silent almost as if waiting expectantly now for the first snows of winter. Then, as we came over the watershed and dropped down to the small bridge spanning the burn from the Dubh Lochan, we became aware of the steady hum of the traffic on the A9, still a full two miles away beyond the Garry. The bridge has had to be considerably renovated, but it is obviously authentic Wade. It jolted us back to reality with a timely reminder of why we were in fact wandering down that road at all. The reminder became plainer still 150 yards further on: a furrow, boulder edged, led down through the heather away from the present road, which makes a wide loop to cross the dip of the Allt Culaibh. We chose to follow Wade, delighted at the prospect of seemingly new discovery. For we knew that the Allt Culaibh would have to be crossed, and I could not remember having read of any bridge over it. Banks of grass and heather hid the last yards to the burn, and we felt like a couple of explorers on the point of some momentous discovery. Sure enough, there it was! The place where Wade's bridge had been — a tumbledown pier on each side of the burn, with, round about, a scattering of boulders of obviously useful shapes and sizes. We were thrilled with our "find", excited as two schoolchildren. It was the perfect climax to all the miles of our walk from Crieff, just the sort of thing, we decided, which made Wade-tracking truly worth while. (And even when, on our return home, we found that after all the bridge is mentioned by the experts, our pleasure was in no way blighted.)

The weather was brightening. As the clouds retreated before the breeze, the afternoon sunshine flooded golden over the birches down on the banks of the Garry; with their more sober greens and browns, the pine woods and moors opposite continued the autumn pageant. More sober still, away through to the west, the mist still half-hid the snowstreaks on the flanks of A'Mharconaich, above Drumochter. It all made up a superb finale for us as we crossed the bridge to the last incline up to the A9.

Perhaps it was just such a day for Wade and his "highwaymen" as they brought this part of their road-making to its conclusion. Perhaps they were into the last hectic days before the end of the season, keeping an anxious watch on the weather-signs as winter threatened to clamp down on further work. However that may have been, we hardly need to be told that they were in the mood to celebrate. Half a dozen miles away, at Oxbridge, the bridge over the Allt Coire Mhic-sith up at Dalnaspidal, there had been a memorable feast when the Dunkeld-Inverness road was completed. Four oxen had been roasted whole, and General Wade himself had been the guest of honour, disclosing afterwards that he was on his feet again in a day or two. Surely it is not unrealistic to suggest that Crieff-Dalnacardoch was celebrated with no less wholehearted abandon.

Heather Track

Suddenly that place rises
Sharp as a stag in my memory.
The track winds round the hillside, out of sight
Like long ago childhood. I see boys going home
With the silver shining of a trout, blue lochs
In their wide-spaced eyes and Gaelic songs
To strengthen the miles of summer midges.
Someone is gathering myrtle, a curlew longs
Over the deep acres of the sky and the lights
Like simple prayers shine out
In the homes that kneel by the loch.

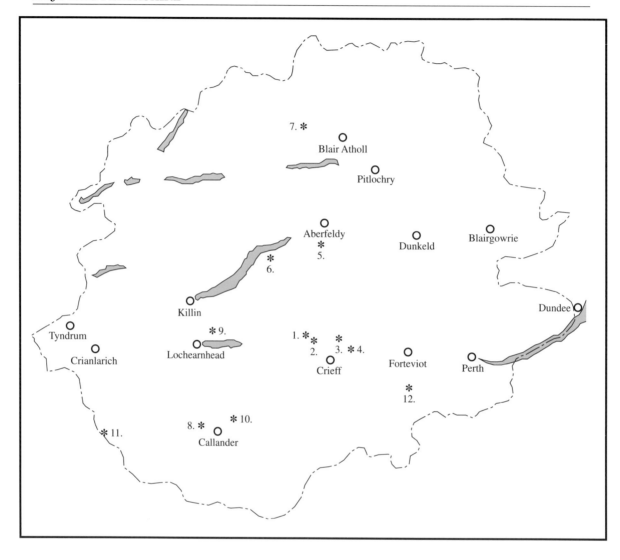

Waterfalls

1.	Falls of Turret	7.	Falls of Bruar
2.	Barvick	8.	Falls of Leny
3.	Keltie	9.	Falls of Beich
4.	Monzie	10.	Bracklinn Falls
5.	Falls of Moness	11.	Beinn Ghlas Falls
6.	Falls of Acharn	12.	Humble Bumble

ENJOYING WATERFALL DAYS

The Camp

Malcolm and myself used to go there
On June days when the dragonflies hummed
And stags lay quiet in the moor's hollows
The sky like brass.

There was a waterfall
Came down from the rocks in a horse's tail
Broke like cream over our bare feet
Cold as ice.

After we swam there like white ghosts
There was always a fire, peat tea
And the dancing glory of the long sun
In the holidays of summer.

ONE VERY real consolation for a disastrously wet summer is the opportunity to enjoy some particularly memorable waterfalling, that worth-while but not so often thought of pastime. The golf course may be virtually unplayable because of casual water, the idea of tennis in oilskins may have singularly little appeal, but at least the addition of a few new, unusually spectacular falls to one's list can be more than a mere second-rate substitute for better things.

There is, of course, no telling in advance which month will be the wettest; Highland weather is never quite so obligingly predictable. For example, August can usually manage to excel itself with some really first-rate flooding, yet Dr Johnson on 30th August 1773, hoping to enjoy seeing the spectacular Fall of Foyers by the side of Loch Ness, complained that it was "divested of its dignity and terror" following "a long continuance of dry weather." Waterfallers, like fishermen, are not the easiest of customers to satisfy.

In Scotland more often than not waterfalls occur on relatively unimportant rivers. The latter are not usually very long, nor do they necessarily drain vast catchment areas. The result is that they have a particularly rapid rise and fall, sensitive to every vagary of the weather. So what, strictly speaking, does constitute a Scottish fall? After a spell of relentless heavy rain every gorge and gully can be foaming angrily white; a hundred different hillsides — up in Torridon, for instance, or on Mull, or round about Fort William — are threaded and streaked by what might easily be classed as genuine waterfalls. Yet it would be safe to predict that within remarkably few hours these same hillsides would be back to their unspectacular normal. So perhaps it is best to acknowledge that there are no cut and dried answers and leave the doubtful falls to be argued about by those so fanatically minded.

For the out-and-out enthusiast Perthshire can provide nothing in the record-breaking category. It has no rival to Scotland's highest, Eas Coul Aulin in Sutherland, with its impressive, abrupt drop of 658 feet, or the thunderous cascade of the Fall of Glomach in Wester Ross, withdrawn behind its none-too-simple approaches. Yet for sheer variety of interest, both on the ground and in associations of various kinds, the county is certainly quite outstanding. With a catalogue of some of Scotland's finest rivers, including Tay and Tummel, Earn and Lyon and Almond, this is perhaps not really surprising. Even the casual waterfaller of today can gain as much honest enjoyment as obviously did the first enquiring tourists of a couple of centuries ago.

One good example of variety of interest is to be found in that quartet of falls — Turret, Barvick, Keltie and Monzie — which may be visited comfortably in a half-day roundabout from Crieff. The four may, of course, be approached and explored in any series of permutations and combinations, but perhaps the sequence which my wife and I followed one bright November afternoon is as enjoyable a pattern as any.

The previous night had brought a sharp drop in temperature with occasional flurries of snow, and up on the rim of the Ben Chonzie plateau the line of sun-touched white suggested the making of the first cornices of winter. There was little wind, however, and it was still pleas-

antly warm walking through the avenue of beeches above the shallow gorge of the Turret. We had left the car near Kiplonie Bridge, off the road which climbs to Loch Turret, to work back along the track on the farther (south-western) bank of the river. It was pleasant going on the deep red carpet of beech leaves, and not many minutes were needed for the quarter mile or so to the rusty old seat which overlooks the river and makes a helpful landmark in the approach to the fall. We had not been that way for some considerable time, and memory tricked me into dropping down to the burn-side beyond the seat, whereas it is advisable to leave the path before it rather than after. A picturesque bridge, ancient-looking and seemingly held together by ferns and sorrel, takes one

A fine 120-ft fall: Black Spout near Pitlochry.

back across the Turret to the north-east bank and the few yards of rock ledge leading to the time-honoured viewpoint in its angle of sheer black walls. The Turret fall itself, some 40 feet high, drops impressively past a dark recess into a partially hidden cauldron, then froths over a further few feet into a quiet mirror pool. For a few minutes we enjoyed renewing acquaintance with it all, then retraced our steps along the ledge and climbed once again up the jungly gully to the path back to Kiplonie Bridge.

For Barvick, second visit of the day, two minutes in the car took us down to the cattle-grid at the foot of the Loch Turret road; thence the familiar 200-yard climb beside the Barvick Burn led easily to a good viewpoint for the falls. The latter consist of two small upper drops, then the main "S" slide of some 30 feet down a groove scoured and polished to glistening ebony. Like every other fall, Barvick can look truly impressive when foaming white in spate; on this November day, at the tail-end of a brief Indian summer, we had to be content with slightly less than its best.

Next on our list was the Keltie Fall, or as it is sometimes called, Sput Ban, the "white spout". There are a number of other "spouts" in the Central Highlands, notably Sput Rolla, the high apron fall spread out across the broad grey rock-face just below the Loch Lednock reservoir, or Buchanty Spout, the well-known salmon leap on the River Almond. Similarly, the Turret Fall which we had just visited has the curious alternative name of Sput Hoick. In this connection, too, it is interesting to call to mind the Red Spout gully in the corrie of that name, Coire Sputan Dearg, on Ben Macdhui, while on the cliffs of Lochnagar there are both a Red Spout and a Black Spout, said in all probability to have been quarries well-known to the old-time gem hunters back in the 1830s.

From the bridge over the Keltie, on the secondary "back" road near Monzie and below Mains of Callander farm, it is a walk of three-quarters of a mile up a pleasant grass-grown track to where the latter finally parts company with the river. Our own way was punctuated with pauses to search for hazel nuts, but the squirrels must have been busy before us, for our efforts met with little success. There was more reward in enjoying the autumn colours — birches still with their scattering of gold, oaks

just beginning to turn, bracken everywhere strikingly patterned in every shade from fading green to russet. At the turn-off point for the fall — a drystane dyke topped with shaky fencing — we headed downhill, flushing a pair of woodcock in passing, then climbed a short way up the bank beyond to a rusty gate on the right. Again bearing right, on a diagonal obstacle course through tumbled bracken and over fallen trees, we reached the edge of the gorge. Unfortunately it was much too overgrown for ideal viewing, although the sheer-sided ravine, plunging into black depths, did allow several impressive glimpses of the fall and made this in fact the most worthwhile of the day's quartet. It is a pity nevertheless that Sput Ban is so awkward to approach, and indeed so little known, for in winter when the trees are bare, it is seen to be a really fine fall, considerably higher than either Turret or Barvick.

Keltie, or Kelty, is a not uncommon name for good-sized, interesting burns. Probably the best-known in Perthshire, apart from the one just mentioned, is the Keltie Water which plunges over the Bracklinn Falls near Callander and, with its chiselled canyon and forbidding black pools, provides such a popular summer-time tourist attraction. There is an interesting note about the name in the Callander parish report contained in the old *Statistical Account*:

Kelty is a name given to rapid waters, in many parts of the world, and in different languages. This name signifies the loss or destruction which these torrents, rising so suddenly, bring on every creature, and every thing in their way. Smooth waters are never called Kelty. There is a Kelty in Strathern, and another in Abyssinia.

Mention might perhaps be made too of another Kelty Water, only a dozen or so miles away from Bracklinn, a burn which rises on the east shoulder of Beinn Bhreac, one of the indeterminate hills behind Balmaha. It flows through the Loch Ard forest, forming a section of the Perthshire-Stirlingshire border, and eventually joins the Forth near Gartmore, between Flanders Moss and Gartrennich Moss.

Presumably to be bracketed with these is Keltney Burn, one of the sources of which is high in the moorland wilderness between Schiehallion and Carn Mairg. Its main course bores through the deep gorge above Coshieville to join the River Lyon at Keltneyburn village. It would be interesting to know for sure the origin of these names. One suggestion is that they are the anglicised form of the Gaelic *coillteach*, meaning "wooded". For example, the River Coiltie, which flows into Loch Ness near Drumnadrochit, has real woodland wealth along its banks, and it is certainly no "smooth water", with the dramatic 100-ft. Divach Falls interrupting its course some 2½ miles upstream from the loch.

In contrast to the Keltie, deep-set in its flank-ing woods, the fourth of our afternoon choices, the Monzie Falls on the Shaggie Burn are simple to locate and reach. They lie an easy quarter of an hour from the main road (A822), along the unsignposted, more westerly of the two tracks half a mile short of Foulford Inn. The fall itself is a modest 35 feet, spilling white over black rock-ledges from the concrete large-bore pipes of an "Irish ford" — no spectacular climax admittedly, but nevertheless a pleasant enough finish to our round in the fading light of a soft November evening.

The falls of Acharn on the south side of Loch Tay.

The Shaggie is another burn which receives interesting mention in the *Statistical Account*, in the Monzie parish report:

In the year 1756, a water spout broke in the hills above Monzie; it took its course down the river Shaggie, and raised it 20 feet perpendicular at the bridge; it swept entirely away a bank near Monzie, which cost 500L. Sterling, and it cast out upon the sides such quantities of fish, that the inhabitants carried them home in baskets; the river subsiding so quickly, that they were left behind.

The week which followed our Crieff roundabout was one of increasing storm. Heavy rain fell, and the autumn trees took a battering which left them tattered and forlorn. It was obvious that the brief fair-weather respite we had been enjoying was now definitely at an end. We had come into a spell of waterfalling weather *par excellence*.

At Aberfeldy, with the Moness Burn chasing to the Tay in boisterous spate, it seemed a pity to miss the chance of paying another visit to the falls a mile up the familiar path at the head of the Birks. Surprisingly, the day of our choice was dry, but a full gale

Moness Falls at the head of the Aberfeldy Birks.

was blowing, and the massed armadas of jackdaws and rooks so often to be heard and seen interweaving in majestic disarray high above the town were exuberantly in their element. Once among the beeches of the Birks car-park it was pleasantly calm, but beside and beyond the footbridge the pounding burn held a note of anger that was not exactly restful; foaming white through its black rock-channel, it had in its hurry the promise of much interest higher up. Now and again we passed quieter reaches, dark and peat-stained, but somehow, with the banks above them carpeted red with fallen beech leaves, they seemed to bear little resemblance to the more familiar golden troutpools of summer.

Burns' seat, in its shallow rock recess beside the path, where the poet is said to have rested on the occasion of his visit to the Den of Moness on 30th August, 1787, is well situated. A few yards beyond it, a sizeable subsidiary fall comes bursting in from the left to join the main stream at the foot of an impressive cascade staircase. Small wonder it is that on that summer day two hundred years ago Burns found in the place his inspiration for *The Birks of Aberfeldy*. Where the verses of the song were actually written is not altogether clear, as the poet wrote later: "I composed these stanzas standing under the Falls of Moness at or near Aberfeldy." One can only hope he was wearing his wet suit at the time!

The poet's seat is in fact only half way to the top of the den and the point at which the well-engineered path starts zigzagging more steeply upwards. Our speed of ascent was not particularly impressive and certainly not helped by the compulsive food-gatherer of the party, who had to be restrained from leaning precariously over the fence to the very edge of the gorge in attempts to reach the best-looking hazel nuts — reminiscent, no doubt, of Edelweiss-hunting days on some of the more perilous slopes of the Alps.

The Moness Fall itself when we reached it was a tremendous sight, an immense volume of water bursting over the rock-lip immediately below the bridge. A full 50 feet in height, the fall was particularly impressive seen through the curtain of fine mist which rose like smoke from the sunless depths of the gorge. Through the drift of spray, indeed, the base of the fall looked doubly distant, and only the familiar fallen tree which lies across the cauldron pool provided a point on which to focus more precisely. I wondered idly how long this gaunt tree skeleton had been lying there, water-polished year in year out, perhaps decade after decade, to an almost sinister slipperiness, black as ebony.

Writing of his visit to the falls during his second tour of Scotland, in 1772, the adventurous Welsh traveller and naturalist Thomas Pennant gives this description:

From the verge of an immense precipice, see another cataract, forming one vast sheet, tumbling into a deep hollow, from which it gushes furiously, and is instantly lost in a wood below. In short Moness is an epitome of all that is admirable in water scenery.

Pennant would certainly have had no reason to change his mind, had he been with us on the day of our visit more than two centuries later.

Our leisurely ascent to the bridge had taken rather more than half an hour; the descent by way of the west side of the gorge took us slightly less. At one point we paused to listen to the whine of the wind in the tree-tops, a reminder of the wild gale still raging in the open; there was ice in its touch, and here and

there so many leaves were falling that they seemed like swirling snow-flurries. Now and again through the birches we could glimpse Farragon on the far side of the strath, its ridges chalky-white with fresh snow. It had been an exhilarating, easy round of exactly 70 minutes.

A further waterfalling attempt several days later met with rather less success. We had for long been intrigued by the name and description of the Humble Bumble. The Humble Bumble is a fall — or perhaps more accurately described as a linn — of which we had heard tell several times and which seemed to call insistently for a visit. It lies on the Water of May, which runs through the Invermay estate near Forteviot, and is some five miles southwest of Perth. We had no difficulty in finding the entrance to the estate beside the bridge over the Water of May, but things went wrong thereafter — we were misdirected and time unfortunately was short. In the end we had to be content with an enjoyable enough walk through attractive woodland — but, sadly, no Humble Bumble; a pity indeed as, even two centuries ago, the linn was considered sufficiently remarkable to be given a worth-while description in the *Statistical Account*:

The water and banks of the May exhibit some natural curiosities, that deservedly attract the attention of strangers. The *Humble Bumble*, in particular, is extremely remarkable. This name is given to a narrow course which the water has cut for itself a considerable way through a rock, the sides of which meet almost together, especially near the top. This passage is both deep and dark. A rumbling noise, which the water makes in its passage through it, is believed to have given rise to the name by which this remarkable place is known. A little above the Humble Bumble is the *Linn of Muckarsey*, about thirty feet perpendicular, which, when the water is high, and comes foaming from the hills, exhibits a beautiful cascade.

Perhaps the Linn of Muckarsey (or Muckersie) would give as good value for a visit as the Bumble, while higher still a tributary of the May which comes in, is a question-mark all on its own; its name — the Kelty Burn! An early winter visit to the much better known Keltie Water, that near Callander, with its tourist showpiece the Bracklinn Falls, was altogether more successful. On our way there we had had glimpses of Ben Voirlich and Stuc a' Chroin, arctic white snow-caps above and beyond the dark foreground of the moors, and as we left the car-park above the town, the barred reds of the sunset and the clearing sky gave promise of another night of frost; ahead, the silver of a threequarter moon was beginning to turn to gold.

It is between half and threequarters of a mile to the falls, and the footprints in the mud of the path told us clearly enough of the popularity of the walk. Beyond the initial stretch of trees, the view opened out over the wide expanse of Flanders Moss and the Carse of Stirling, with a horizon sweep of low hills, a black silhouette from the edge of the Ochils round to Dumgoyne, unmistakably outlined against the furnace of the sunset. Long before we reached the deep trough of the burn, we could hear the sound of the falls, carried towards us on the gentle east wind. Then it grew louder as we dropped down the steps to the metal footbridge across the narrow neck of the gorge. The falls above this are broad rather than high, perhaps not so much typically Highland as suggestive of some limestone showpiece of the Yorkshire Dales. But the scattering of immense rock-slabs, as if sliced and chiselled and squared by some mason of the Titans, makes a setting that is surely quite unique. And downstream from the bridge, plunging rock-walls scarred and scooped by floodwater, enclose deep, dark pools in an astonishing, almost startling sequence. The rocky bluffs beyond the bridge must make ideal picnic spots in summer — though not, we decided, with toddlers roaming free.

As we climbed the steps once again and made our way back to the car, shafts of the sunset's gold still made a brilliant pattern of the oaks bordering the gorge and deepened the rich purple bloom of the leafless birches, as if highlighting finally this visit to remember. The only unanswered question, it seemed to me, was why we had never been there before. The *Statistical Account* certainly underlines clearly enough the impressiveness of Bracklinn. Nowadays it is good to have the reassurance of the bridge; two centuries ago it would all have been very different; hardly a friendly place in times of spate:

In the glen betwixt Brackland and Achinlaich,

there is a bridge on the water of Kelty, consisting of 2 sticks, covered with a few branches of trees and some turf, which is abundantly romantic and dangerous. The sticks are laid across the chasm, with their ends resting on the rocks, which project on opposite sides, about 50 feet high, above a deep pool. On the one hand, the white cascade precipitates itself, from a height above the bridge, with a tremendous noise, occasioned by the conflict of the rocks, the narrowness of the passage, and the lofty column of water, whose spray often wets the clothes of passengers. On the other hand, the winding glen, which deepens as it descends, the gloominess of the hanging rocks, of the shading trees, and black pools, strikes with terror and with awe. Yet the people of the adjacent farms, from the mere force of habit, pass and repass with very little concern; although the very act of looking down, when there is a flood in the water, must fill the head of a stranger with a swimming giddiness, owing to the altitude of his situation, the deafening roar of the torrent, the gloomy horror of the glen, and the whirling of the pool below, into which the cascade falls, rolling, tossing, thundering down.

On the other side of Callander, two miles to the west beside the A84, the Falls of Leny lure innumerable summer visitors along the short path to grandstand vantage-points above the river. For height the falls are unremarkable — unless maybe to the autumn salmon fighting their way upstream to spawn. Yet during a time of angry spate the rapids, surging and tossing in their twin channels round the central island of tilted brown rock, are always worth seeing. One February visit is especially memorable: it had been a day of much rain on a warm west wind and the light was failing with the early dusk. For a while we stood looking down, half-hypnotised by the frenzy of water swollen with melting snow from high on Ben Ledi. I remember thinking, rather unromantically, that the noise and vibration suggested nothing so much as the sudden earth-shaking clangour of one of the night sleepers from Euston pounding and swaying at speed, northbound through Watford Junction.

Much less accessible and so, I imagine, comparatively rarely visited, is an interesting fall on the Beich Burn, which drops down to the

One of the falls in the gorge of the River Bruar. **(George Thomson, LRPS)**

selves by wondering, including some of the same ones we had seen earlier on in Norway at the tail-end of summer. The track beyond Glenbeich Lodge leads to a wooden bridge over a tributary burn tumbling in picturesquely from the left — probably the fall marked on the old Stobie's map of 1783, although not the one we were looking for. In fact no fall at all is shown on the latest Ordnance Survey 1 : 50 000 sheet, and Mais and I were all but defeated in our search. We walked too far and had to retrace our steps, keeping more closely to the edge of the gorge of the main Beich Burn to a point a quarter of a mile or so beyond the wooden bridge just mentioned. There, finally, it was below us, magnificently explosive. We calculated its height as 60 feet, although that was open to a niggle of doubt, as the fall spills from a narrow recess and is awkward to see really well from the west bank, where we stood; doubly so as we found it, with the sloping turf underfoot treacherously frost-glazed. A splendid fall, we decided, if needing more time than we could spare to find a wholly satisfying viewpoint for it.

Another Perthshire fall which was one of the earliest we visited was Acharn. Situated on the burn of that name, which drops into Loch Tay a mile and a half south-west of Kenmore, it had been commended to us by an enthusiastic waterfalling friend as being a vertical fall "comparatively little known and relatively secluded; well worth seeking out, not least for its romantic setting." Our expectations were high.

On the day of our first visit we approached the loch by way of the high pass over from Glen Quaich, the strong winter sunshine making glittering snowshields of the Lawers outliers and the rounded hills of Glen Lyon. From the village cluster of Acharn a gritty Land-Rover track climbs steeply beside the deep, sunless gorge of the burn, and this we followed to the airy van-

north side of Loch Earn two miles from Lochearnhead. Glen Beich slants far back into the untidy hinterland of moorland hills between Loch Earn and Loch Tay, and so beautiful was the early winter morning when my wife and I started up it, that we were strongly tempted by the completely impracticable idea of walking the eight miles through to Ardeonaig. The sky was alpine blue, the rust of the dead bracken offset high up by a carpeting of fresh snow immaculately white in the sun-glint. Scores of fieldfares and redwings were restlessly on the move in the fields — maybe, we amused our-

tage-point directly opposite the fall itself, a semi-natural "belvedere" stance, reached through several yards of rock-tunnelling. With the trees bare, we had an excellent view of the fall across the intervening dark depths of the den. Our hopes had certainly been high, as the Tay was in full flood at the time and we had noted on the map that up on the moors the sources of the Acharn Burn itself are not far below the 3,000-foot level. Nor were we disappointed: the fall plunges over a steep-sided face of black, polished rock, curling at first through a restricted groove, then dropping free for some 55 feet to a final 20-foot sequence of stepped runnels. It makes a splendid sight, particularly impressive when the burn is in really heavy spate.

The belvedere or gazebo opposite the fall has been in existence for over two centuries. It is mentioned in the enthusiastic write-up of Richard Joseph Sulivan, Esq., a gentleman traveller from South of the Border, in 1778. In his *Tour through Different Parts of England, Scotland and Wales* he says:

> About one mile from Taymouth lies the Hermitage; a deep dell on the southern side of the loch, down which a huge stream rolls from a prodigious height in awful majesty, bursting over heaps of misshapen rocks, and sprinkling the forest trees, which profusely sprout around it.

Later, in 1825, *The Scottish Tourist* notes that "a hermitage, with appropriate decorations, has been reared in the vicinity of the waterfall."

Our approach to Kenmore over the hill from Glen Quaich was the same as that followed by Burns when, on 29th August, 1787, he travelled from Crieff to Taymouth. It would seem that in his day graffiti was as much in fashion as it is now, for at Kenmore inn the poet got busy with his pencil over the chimney-piece:

Admiring Nature in her wildest grace,
These northern scenes with weary feet I trace;
O'er many a winding dale and painful steep,
Th'abodes of coveyed grouse and timid sheep,
My savage journey, curious, I pursue,
Till fam'd Breadalbane opens to my view. .....

And these further lines suggest more specifically that during his brief stay he managed to fit in a visit to Acharn:

Poetic ardours in my bosom swell,
Lone wandering by the hermit's mossy cell:
The sweeping theatre of hanging woods;
Th'incessant roar of headlong tumbling floods.

Above the fall and some 50 yards below the old bridge taking the track across the burn, a path cuts down the grassy bank of the den. It is well worth following, as it leads to a fine chain of dark pools, scooped and scalloped by countless spinning floods. Two wooden bridges, quite recently built by the officers and men of 202 Field Squadron Royal Engineers, make a picturesque crossing to the east bank, where a track, pleasantly vague to start with, drops down through an impressive mix of oak and ash, beech and birch, to the houses of Acharn village.

On the west side of the burn also there have been recent developments, with much tree planting between the track and the sharp drop into the den. The profusion of oaks, beeches and geans will no doubt delight many visitors of the future; looking back, it is not difficult to imagine how pleased Burns would have been to add to his effusion on Acharn a compliment or two about this particularly worth-while work.

Burns certainly was a most enthusiastic waterfaller. In the course of his 600-mile tour of the Central Highlands in August-September, 1787, he carried his Journal in his pocket and wrote it up as occasion permitted — perhaps, also, when his concentration was not disturbed by his irascible, quarrelsome schoolmaster companion William Nicol. We learn from his notes that he visited Cauldron Linn, Rumbling Bridge and the Deil's Mill on the Perthshire-Kinross-shire border; possibly Acharn; the Moness Falls at Aberfeldy; the Hermitage on the Braan, near Dunkeld; Killiecrankie; Tilt Falls and the Falls of Bruar. A list which could hardly have been improved upon.

It was while he was staying at Blair Castle at the beginning of September, 1787, that Burns visited Bruar and composed "the effusion of a half-hour" — *The Humble Petition of Bruar Water to the Noble Duke of Athole*. Among the eleven verses of the poem the following two are perhaps the most apt:

Here, foaming down the skelvy rocks,
In twisting strength I rin;
There, high my boiling torrent smokes,
Wild-roaring o'er a linn:

Enjoying large each spring and well
As Nature gave them me,
I am, altho' I say't mysel,
Worth gaun a mile to see.

Would then my noble master please
To grant my highest wishes,
He'll shade my banks wi' towering trees,
And bonie spreading bushes.
Delighted doubly then, my Lord,
You'll wander on my banks,
And listen mony a grateful bird
Return you tuneful thanks.

The humble petition was certainly heeded. Some ten years after Burns' visit, John Murray, Fourth Duke of Atholl, ("Planter John") put in 15 million larch trees in more than 10,000 acres of plantations on his estates. Many of these were obviously set out on the banks of the Bruar, for another 30 years later, in 1825, the author of *The Scottish Tourist* commented: "The poetical prayer of the Bruar, to have its banks shaded with trees, has been complied with by the Duke of Atholl; but years must intervene before the improvements of his Grace produce their proper effect." A considerable number of trees were felled during World War II, although there was subsequent tree-planting with Scots pine and hybrid larch. Natural regeneration of birch, rowan, aspen, willow and conifers such as spruce and fir has also helped. Today there are those who would contend that the round by the Falls of Bruar may be claimed to provide the most picturesque waterfall walk in Perthshire. Indeed, thanks to the part played by this rich variety of trees clustering to the steep sides of the gorge, the walk may certainly be said to rival the pinewoods of Speyside or some of the quiet corners of Norway or the Tyrol.

Buchanty Spout, well-known salmon leap on the River Almond.

When we first visited Bruar, it was one of those mornings of early summer which seem almost too good to be true. The trees beside the car-park and the bridge over the river were loud with the songs of willow-warblers and chaffinches; as we started up the path a particularly vociferous wren kept chiming in merrily from the farther bank of the burn. It was a walk of little more than ten minutes to the lower falls and bridge but if there had been any thoughts of speed up until this point, they certainly lasted no longer. Colour had characterised the approaches — greys of rock-walls patchy with lichens and heather-clumps, greens of conifers, browns and flecked whites of the burn itself. The fall immediately above the bridge — not high, but curling attractively into a pool that on a day of sunshine reflects the sky's blue — is well seen from a platform viewpoint. Here is a parting of the ways: one can follow either side of the gorge according to choice as far as the higher footbridge just above the upper, main falls. Both halves of the track are splendidly engineered and well maintained; indeed, back in 1803, William Wordsworth seems to have objected to the fact that they were too tidy — "brushed neatly without a blade of grass or a weed upon them." We followed the left, west-side path and returned down the east, both tracks through the pines and birches and rowans a rich mixture of sunshine and shadow. We had been concerned on the way up that we had had no good glimpses of the main falls, but there was ample recompense looking back a quarter of a mile or so down the east, return track: this is the classic view, with an excellent, if fairly distant, impression of the fine 50-foot drop and the four minor falls immediately above. Like many more august visitors before us, including Queen Victoria herself — although we did not, like her, "throw stones down to see the effect in the water" — we were memorably impressed. Without further delay we rattled down to the lower bridge and the last rather muddy stretch of path above the car-park. The round of just under two miles had taken us a little more than a leisurely hour.

Quite apart from its attractiveness, Bruar intrigued me on account of its name, and that in rather a roundabout way. During the war I had spent three months in various parts of Iceland and as a result had come to be more than ordi-

narily interested in that country. Outstanding among Iceland's scenic attractions are its waterfalls — Dettifoss, Godafoss, Gullfoss, Skogafoss, Oxararfoss and others, household names to any Icelander and some, indeed, well known the world over. One fall with which I was familiar by name was Bruarfoss, in south-west Iceland, and it struck me as more than a little strange that there should be a "foss" in Iceland called exactly the same as one in the heart of Perthshire. Somehow, I felt sure, there must be an interesting link. "Bru" in Norwegian is a bridge, and "Bruar" I discovered in a dictionary of Scottish place-names refers to natural rock bridges — the key to the puzzle, surely, as there is an excellent example of one such arch to be seen at the lower falls on the Perthshire Bruar, and there may possibly be more higher up in the deep trough of the burn, unseen from the path. The question then appeared to be: was there similarly a natural bridge across the river in Iceland? I could find no picture or description of Bruarfoss in my books on Iceland; the travel agency in Reykjavik to which I appealed could do no better than invite me to visit the "Land of Ice and Fire". The quest seemed to have come to an unsatisfactory conclusion. But there was a happier ending in store: our good friend Gunnar Godwin, with his close Icelandic associations, was able to provide the answer. Formerly there had indeed been a natural rock bridge over the river at Bruarfoss. Across this — according to legend — had dashed a criminal fleeing hot foot from justice. Very conveniently the bridge had collapsed behind him, leaving him safe from his pursuers. A pleasantly colourful story and not one which our Perthshire Bruar can come anywhere near matching.

Yet the puzzle of when and how the actual name originated in Atholl remained to be solved. According to the Blair Castle archives, it first appears in records at the end of the 17th century, although it may well have been known before that time. So far as the Scandinavian influence is concerned, this was ruled out absolutely by a place-name expert at the School of Scottish Studies in Edinburgh. His suggestion was rather that the derivation is from the early Celtic, Bruar representing a "Brivaros" or "Brivara" (pronounced "Bruaros" or "Bruara") meaning "bridge-stream". This, he said, would date from the days when "bridge-streams" were quite common, the bridges being often crude rows of boulders thrown across the rivers to provide makeshift crossings, for example for pack-horses.

Such, of course, may indeed be the true answer to the problem; far be it from a mere enthusiastic amateur to quibble. Yet it is difficult to feel entirely satisfied that this explains fully so curious a link between Perthshire and Iceland.

Another fall which holds a special place in more distant memory lies well to the west of Bruar, at the foot of Glen Falloch, precisely on the boundary between Perthshire and Dunbartonshire. There, the Beinn Ghlas Falls hang strikingly on the steep hillside across the glen. When seen in heavy spate, the falls can look truly dramatic; on the other hand, in summer droughts the flow of water can shrink to a thread, leaving a bare, slabby staircase which has even provided an interesting rock-climbing route on at least one occasion. The path beside the falls, starting behind Beinn Ghlas farm, can be the gateway to great things: back in 1803, for William and Dorothy Wordsworth, accompanied

Rock architecture in the gorge of the River Bruar.

by Coleridge, it was the prelude to their long walk over the watershed of Scotland and down by Loch Katrine to the Trossachs; for humbler individuals in rather more recent times, it is the frequent approach to the southernmost of the Crianlarich hills, often enough on winter mornings when bitter frost has half-tamed the venom of the falls and set icicles dangling from every rock-lip and ledge.

Yet although it is good to recall days that are past, one can look pleasurably too to the future. For most of us there are always likely to be more worth-while waterfalls in Perthshire still to be "discovered", even if, needless to say, these may vary in impressiveness according to the eye of the beholder and probably even more according to weather vagaries.

A thoroughly useful guide to the whole range of possibilities is Mr Louis Stott's book *The Waterfalls of Scotland,* * comprehensive and superbly illustrated. In his section covering the Tay and Earn basins more than 60 different falls and linns are listed, so there is certainly no good excuse for failing to enjoy that aspect of outdoors Perthshire.

Yet it would not be altogether kindly to add suggestion to suggestion, for at least half the fun of a pastime such as waterfalling lies in making discoveries for oneself. Perthshire is a large county. Ideal waterfalling weather is rarely likely to be lacking. Good maps and a modicum of leisure are the only other incentives needed to persuade one to be up and doing.

The Linn

This is a day for the river
For descending through the lime and lemon trees,
The path's oven-hot sand
To sudden blue water.

At that point it comes down the rocks
In white wings, jumbles into a deep pool
Struggles out sideways through branches and rocks
Into the woods.

Children come here all summer
Tarzan from rocks, crash out into pools
Slash water at each other, needle and thread
In chases between the trees.

At night the barbecues are lit
Lanterns like moons hung from the branches
And the air smells of thunder and meat
The first hay jade in the fields behind.

* *Aberdeen University Press (1987).*

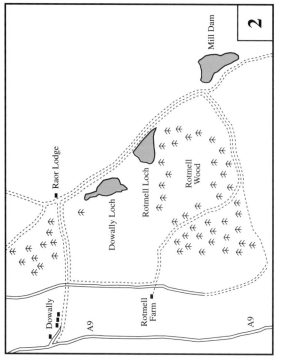

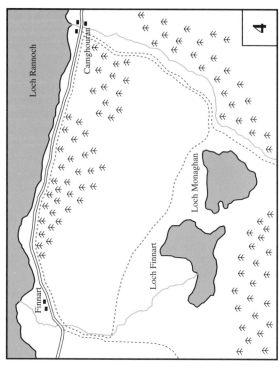

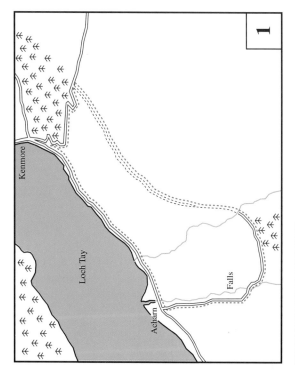

"FIVE MILERS"

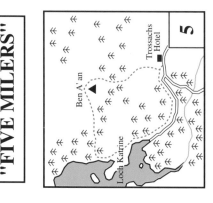

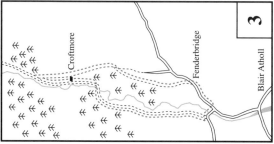

ENJOYING FAMILY "FIVE-MILERS"

For Life Itself

Thank you for reason to laugh
To catch the river in both hands, to be a child again
To storm new-fallen chestnuts, count the stars
To chase through gold-thatched autumn fields
To watch with burning eyes the lightning's horses
Bells of rain for singing. Thank you for breathlessness
Tiredness, days fuller than a stream in salmon flood
For sharing when the world was beautiful
Life's light with me.

BEACH-COMBING and sea-cliff strolling apart, Perthshire is able to offer as rich a variety of walks as any county in Scotland. Making the round of some of the smaller lochs like Loch Turret or Loch Freuchie; exploring the forest trails of Craigvinean or Drummond Hill; following the riverside bends of Lyon, or Earn, or Almond — there is no end to suggestion and counter-suggestion, combination and permutation.

Much of our own family's enjoyment derives from "lazy man's choices" — half-day walks of five miles or thereabouts, followed more often than not because we have been too disorganised to plan anything more ambitious in advance. Not indeed that longer outings have always been noteworthy for success: for example, the eleven-mile walk from Corrour to Rannoch station, across the edge of Rannoch Moor, was a disaster of relentless rain, an encounter with an interminable succession of swirling, swollen burns. Other treks too, such as that over the pass from Inverarnan and down Glen Gyle and the side of Loch Katrine, or through upper Glen Almond from Newton Bridge to Loch Tay-side, have needed fairly elaborate transport arrangements — the kind of expeditions which are not just the result of flustered decisions taken half way through a Saturday morning.

Yet it is to be hoped that the details of a few unambitious, scarcely historic, achievements may set other families on their way to finding what we have found so often — a real sense of satisfaction out of all proportion to the number of miles covered.

★　★　★

AS WE LEFT the car high above Kenmore on the road climbing up over the hill to Glen Quaich and Amulree, we were given immediate greeting by a golden eagle soaring and swinging above the moorland flank of Creag an Fhudair. For several minutes we watched it circling lazily in the thermals, drifting gradually higher without a single wing-beat, till finally it was away, lost to sight in the distance somewhere towards Acharn. Then we turned to the business in hand.

The business was in fact an exploratory visit to the old track which runs temptingly westwards, 500 feet above Loch Tay, from the gate at the upper edge of the woods. It could, we decided, lead into a "five-star" circular walk of almost exactly five miles.

It was a bitingly cold day of early November, with the feel of snow in the boisterous north-east wind. Overnight frost had left a skin of ice on the puddles of the track. But the sun shone and as we looked west along the steely furrow of Loch Tay, all was right with the world: Ben Lawers alpine white, its east ridge a knife-edge between sunlit snow-flank and shadowed corrie; Meall Greigh, which we had climbed only a few weeks earlier, a humbler alpine neighbour; Drummond Hill, just across the valley, a pattern

In Glen Tilt: the Bedford memorial bridge.

of green pines and rusty larches; Kenmore at our feet a neat picture postcard. Clearly this was the right direction in which to do the walk, east to west — looking all the time to the superb best of the views.

Regretfully, however, lack of time forced us to call it a day. At the point where the track enters a straggling birch wood we turned and made back to the car. But we knew that a return visit could not be long delayed.

In fact, we managed to fit in the full walk only a few days later. This time we parked the car on the main road down by the loch-side, half a mile from Acharn towards Kenmore, the object of this being to do first the low-level stretch of the walk and the unavoidable climb from Kenmore while we were still fresh. That went pleasantly well. Along by the shore we were sheltered from the wind, which did its best to nag us maliciously from behind; on the long, zigzag climb — so widely known once as a motor-cycle test hill — we exulted in the woods aflame with the

autumn colouring, a magnificent winding corridor of birch and rowan, oak and hazel and occasional Spanish chestnut. Yet it was a long enough upward plod, and by the time we had reached the gate at the top we were not too sorry to pause for our sandwich lunch.

Unfortunately the weather was not as impeccable as it had been on our previous visit. True, we started along the track in the smile of a sunblink that heightened the colouring of Kenmore at our feet and Drummond Hill beyond. But we could see trouble in store: Lawers hidden in indigo cloud, snow-curtains drifting on the wind across the jaws of Glen Lyon.

It hit us just beyond the birch wood — cold, wet sleet flung in our faces on half a gale. Heads down we battled uncomfortably against it, soon damp as passengers in a speedboat cowering against the spray of an angry sea. There was no shelter anywhere near, and with a cheerless grey void ahead, we could only decide we had seen the end of enjoyment for the day.

Near the summit of Carn Liath, one of the three Beinn a' Ghlo Munros.

On the lochside road near the Black Wood of Rannoch.

But we were wrong. Half way between the wood and the old farm buildings of Balmacnaughton the sun began to struggle through. The wind eased and the sleet slackened to gentler misty rain. Schiehallion emerged from behind a rainbow. Soon, thankfully, we were beginning to dry off in bright afternoon warmth.

Beyond the farm the way is not obvious. We chose to keep at a low level across the fields and realised too late that we had chosen wrongly. The correct direction is a slightly uphill slant for perhaps 250 yards to an excellent footbridge across the Allt Mhucaidh, a burn which — in our stupidity — gave us quite enough trouble just to teeter across from stone to stone and which in spate might well have been impassable.

Beyond, however, we were on course again — hardly difficult, as from the bridge there is a track fit for Land-Rovers. Skirting a wood past a conspicuous big barn, we reached in less than half a mile the gorge of the Acharn Burn, a dark slot with here and there the scarlet splash of rowans. Thereafter the track followed pleasantly downhill to more familiar territory — the bridge not far above the Acharn Falls. We turned aside briefly through the rock "burrow" to the hermitage vantage-point, enjoying as always the dramatic view of the falls; then off down the winding lane to the village.

Meanwhile the sun had gone in once more.

Over the loch towards Lawers and Meall Greigh the weather was greying up. We lost no time in completing the final half mile back along the main road. Exactly as we reached the car the rain hit us again, cold and venomous as before. We had had the best of the day. With all our dawdling and all our burn-crossing folly, the round had taken us just two and three-quarter hours.

★　★　★

UP ON the hillsides above Dowally, the little village cluster on the A9 three miles south of Ballinluig, there is a network of lanes and quiet tracks pre-eminently worth getting to know. Here it was that Queen Victoria managed to find herself in moderately deep trouble in the pitch darkness and driving rain of an October evening in 1865. Nearing the end of one of her marathon coach-drives — on this occasion from Braemar to Dunkeld by way of Glenshee, Strathardle and ten miles of open moorland — the coachman missed the way coming down from Loch Ordie. They strayed on to "a track for carting wood" and just managed to make progress with one of the attendants walking ahead with a lantern. Further on "the road was very rough, and we had to go through some deep holes full of water." In the end all was well, though we can imagine that the 9.30 p.m. dinner in the Duchess of Athole's "nice, snug little cottage" at Dunkeld was a particularly welcome affair.

The lonely track up to Loch Ordie is not the only choice above Dowally. Another excellent expedition — a modest four miles — is through to Loch of Craiglush. This in turn can be varied in its later stages to lead down to Dunkeld itself, with maybe a diversion to the Loch of the Lowes visitor centre as an additional bonus at the end of the day. Unfortunately an obvious drawback to following this route right through from end to end is the need for two-car collaboration, and as an alternative our family has several times chosen a circular walk of five equally un-strenuous miles — a round to be recommended particularly warmly.

Probably our most memorable visit was on a day of early May. A night of surprisingly hard frost had given way to one of those mornings of cloudless sunshine which put one to shame for

not having been up and out with the dawn. For the first, wooded, half mile above Dowally chaffinches and willow-warblers seemed to be vying with each other in the exuberance of their welcomes, all against the background undertones of the burn. We were glad all the same to reach the higher, more open stretch leading to Raor Lodge, where the track to Loch Ordie veers off uphill to the left.

Knowing the good things in store, we had no difficulty in resisting the temptation of the higher moors, bearing off right-handed instead, full into the sun. In a couple of hundred yards we were alongside the sparkle of Dowally Loch, first of the three lochs which "make" this section of the walk. Down on the shore by the outflow burn a sandpiper was voicing its agitation. On the far bank two fishermen were no doubt eyeing the dazzle on the water with disfavour and hoping despondently for rain.

Rotmell Loch, second in the chain, has an excellent grandstand beside it — a jumble of giant blocks fallen from a line of crags — and we were well content to pause for lunch in a particularly sunny corner. A small party of wigeon had taken off in disarray from an inlet opposite as soon as we had appeared, but half a dozen "tufties" and a pair of Canada geese were still in view apparently unconcerned. A cuckoo decided to call tantalisingly in the distance and a curlew flew calling over the rough ground behind the far edge of the loch. Somewhere up in the crags behind us a ring-ouzel was chattering from time to time, sadly preferring to be heard but not seen.

Beyond Rotmell the track continues to the third of the lochs, the Mill Dam, and runs pleasantly alongside the latter for its full length before dropping down gradually to Loch of Craiglush. Over the years the Mill Dam has given us many good days, usually following an approach from the opposite, southern side and a visit to the Loch of the Lowes. It is popular with fishermen and there are often one or two boats out. This seems, however, to cause little disturbance to the bird life in and around the reedy no-man's-land at the northern end. Indeed the disturbance is more likely to be the other way round, as the most numerous inhabitants are scores of blackheaded gulls, an angry, hostile, vociferous throng, never anything but thoroughly restless and unwelcoming. It is as well nevertheless not to allow the gulls to be too distracting, for there are always interesting sightings to reward patience and a stealthy approach. A pair or two of wigeon are usually to be seen, teal now and again, and once in nesting time a really surprise "bonus" of a drake pintail. Moorhens and coots skulk, while, more bravely obvious, there are usually Canada geese and great-crested grebes out on the loch itself.

Unfortunately, on our May morning round walk, we were slightly short of time. Our route branched uphill to the right 100 yards or so before the Mill Dam's swampy fringe, and although we did deviate for a quick look, we had no rewards of any interest. The gulls, of course, did not like us — and told us so, emphatically. Screaming and screeching, they took wing in an untidy, abusive slanging match, impatient to see the last of us.

We turned to the uphill slant and behind us the clamour gradually died. Bare slopes gave way to a plantation, where a pair of whinchats seemed scarcely more welcoming than the gulls had been. This was the start of a different section of the walk, a line still vaguely uphill cutting through the massed conifers of Rotmell Wood. We met a couple who told us that they had had an excellent view of a cock capercaillie in one of the rides, but we had no such good fortune, our own incidents to remember being provided by an adder going our way along the dusty track, a family of siskins noisily busy among the spruces, and two or three goldcrests, unseen among Christmas tree branches, their quick whisperings insistent on territorial rights.

Again the path was downhill and again the background changed, this time to more open woodland — oaks and beeches, scattered and stately, suggesting perhaps the corner of some walkway in the Yorkshire Dales. Sadly the day had lost its sparkle. Clouds had been gathering, crowding in from the west. Over the Tummel valley by Pitlochry and beyond, they had already massed to a uniform slate grey. We pressed on more quickly over the last mile, alongside the fields of Rotmell Farm, where the peewits were crying. Then we rejoined our track of the morning and went down, glad enough of sheltering trees once more. The wind was rising and before we reached the car the

Loch Tay and the Ben Lawers group from the track above Kenmore.

rain had begun in earnest. No doubt the fishermen up at Dowally Loch would be rejoicing.

★ ★ ★

LIKE THE crossing of the Corrieyairack or the linking of Speyside and Deeside by way of the Lairig Ghru, the walk through Glen Tilt is one of the classic expeditions of the Highlands. Whether taken from north to south, from the Linn of Dee to Blair Atholl, or in the opposite direction, following the example of such illustrious travellers as Thomas Pennant or Queen Victoria, it is a marathon never likely to be forgotten.

From the Linn of Dee, past White Bridge and the ruins of Bynack Lodge, to the watershed and county boundary near Loch Tilt is seven miles; continuing on the Perthshire side, down the glen itself to Bridge of Tilt, it is all of a further fourteen. Thus, to appreciate the walk fully, a whole day — and usually a deal of head-scratching over transport problems — is needed. Yet to give up the idea of "discovering" Glen Tilt — surely one of the finest half dozen glens in Scotland — simply because of the length of such an expedition, would be sad indeed.

My own first taste was in 1955, when on a perfect June evening Carn a' Chlamain, seven miles up the glen, gave me of its best. A quarter of a century later the same Munro provided a good family day after a chilly night's camping near Gilbert's Bridge. Between these two outings, the rich filling of this sandwich was a memorable May walk in 1967 right through the glen from the Linn of Dee.

A much more recent November afternoon saw my wife and me start a five-mile round at Fenderbridge, a mile

above Blair Atholl. It was an almost unbelievably good day for the time of year — sunny and mild, with a gentle south-west breeze — and we decided we would gladly have been embarking on the entire public footpath trek through to Deeside. Beyond the first fields with their far views the track had a Wade-like quality about it, running through an avenue of birches and later more darkly crowding larches. For the most part the birches were leafless and showing to advantage their winter mulberry, their fallen leaves and the larch needles a scattering of gold

Looking up Loch Katrine from the summit of Ben A'an

and copper all along the path. Below and well down to our left, we could hear the deep bass accompaniment of the Tilt. Once we paused to watch a bullfinch family on the move above the track; ahead of us a pair of roe deer hurried across into the thicker sanctuary of the larches. On the more open hillside beyond the wood a kestrel was busy hunting, hovering for a hopeful half-minute, then suddenly swinging away unsatisfied to the far side of the river.

We carried on for rather less than a mile, then stopped for lunch on a grassy bank looking down to the Tilt a short distance past Gilbert's Bridge, so named to commemorate William Gilbert Robertson, who was "out" during the Forty-Five. (Other interestingly named bridges in the glen are the Shepherd's Bridge or Drochaid na Roineag, the "bridge of sheep's wool", and, higher up towards the watershed, the Bedford suspension bridge, named after Francis John Bedford, aged 18, who was drowned in a nearby pool in 1879.)

There was an attractive look about the further reaches of the glen, twisting north-eastwards below the sunlit chocolate and gold of Carn a' Chlamain, and we were sorely tempted to continue even for a mile or two more, a worth-while addition to any short round such as ours. But we had reached our agreed turning-point and, besides, our walk back by the Tilt itself was to be no mere second-rate alternative. A short-cut past a sheep fank took us quickly down to the main glen road beside the river.

It would be good to know precisely the origin and meaning of the name Tilt. According to the old *Statistical Account*, Te-allt is the "warm rivulet", so called from its sheltered, warm banks. Hardly a convincing interpretation. Yet even the late Professor W.J. Watson in his classic *History of the Celtic Place-Names of Scotland* admits that "the meaning is obscure to me." My own theory, which doubtless to the expert is merely laughable, is that the name is a combination of *tuil*, "flood" or "deluge" and *allt*, "mountain stream". In wild spate conditions it must indeed be a sight to remember.

I had certainly forgotten how impressive it can be. Even after the unusually dry autumn weather we had been having, it was no disappointment — rock-slides and rapids, eddies and overflows, grey-ledged pools, white-flecked and peat-stained; such was the succession, half-forgotten yet delighting afresh. Only yards beyond the road-edging of planted beeches, it kept close company with us along the short stretch to Gilbert's Bridge itself. Thereafter it continued below us, deeper in a grey canyon-scoop where the rock had been cut and carved and chiselled by the malevolence of a thousand floods.

The section of road we were to follow was hardly as spectacular as that higher up the glen: for Thomas Pennant in 1769 "the most dangerous and the most horrible I have ever travelled;" for the author of *The Scottish Tourist* in 1825, a track "passing along the brink of fearful precipices which rise from the bed of the river." Yet in its own way it had much to contribute to a memorable second half of the walk. Cutting at first through youngish conifers, heady-scented and exhilarating, it passed below the house and garden of Croftmore, then curved into a valley through more mature woodland. This in turn took us to a narrowing of the river and a crossing to the west bank.

At the bridge a family party of long-tailed tits cheerfully on the move had us pausing briefly to enjoy their exuberant chit-chat, setting us thinking of the medley of bird-song there would be in spring in the mixed woodland just ahead. Then, as we dropped down finally to the Old Bridge of Tilt, we were skirting more open parkland — spacious fields with islands of tall larches, where mistle thrushes ranted at us, seemingly as ill-tempered as the pair of buzzards which were mewing overhead. On the bridge we took a final look at the river below, then set off up the last half mile to Fenderbridge and the car. We had been away for a leisurely 2¾ hours.

It had been good to savour Glen Tilt once again, even if our sortie had done little more than provide a brief nibble at the cake. There had been much to remind us of brave days long past: the far ridges above the curve of the glen; the autumn tints of the woods we had been through; the music of the river as it spun and swirled over its polished rock-shelves. Indeed there was no least difficulty in sharing more than a little of what Queen Victoria must have felt as she wrote up her Journal after the long miles of her ride through to Deeside: "This was the pleasantest and most enjoyable expedition I *ever* made; and the recollection of it will always be most agreeable to me, and increase my wish to make more!" Remarkable evidence surely of the Queen's stamina as well as of her huge enjoyment of the glen. "Did not feel tired," she noted in the same journal entry. Yet she had travelled 69 miles that day and 60 the day before, much of the way on pony-back.

Which did not really leave us any excuse for feeling weary after our rather more modest round.

★   ★   ★

FROM the scattering of houses at Camghouran, some 2¹/₂ miles from the west end of Loch Rannoch, a Land-Rover track wanders off, vaguely southwards, into the hills. On the one hand, according to the map, is the "big wood", Coille Mhor; on the other, the western fringe of the Black Wood of Rannoch. The track itself, pleasantly uphill to begin with, follows closely along the bank of the Allt Camghouran.

Our first visit was on a winter's day of brilliant sun-dazzle, with, underfoot, several inches of crisp snow, so that we found ourselves wishing for cross-country skis. As it was, our only show of winter sporting prowess was when the younger members of the party enjoyed an hour of first-rate sliding on the ice of Loch Monaghan, hard frozen in its exposed moorland saucer. We looked forward to returning and to the trying out of a worth-while five-mile circuit.

Back in the early eighteenth century the village of Camghouran was, surprisingly, home to a fair-sized colony of members of Clan Cameron, obviously immigrants from the Lochaber side of Rannoch Moor. Their days are recalled by the number of Cameron tombstones, askew with age and barely legible, crowded in the secluded little graveyard not far from the shore of Loch Rannoch. After Culloden the clansmen apparently found the nearby Black Wood a highly useful hideout; a century later there was no escape at all: the village was cleared to make way for sheep.

We chose another winter morning, the last day of January. Again the sunshine was unbroken, the sky gentian blue. This time, however, there was much less snow, with Schiehallion's north face as we passed zebra-striped rather than carpeted white to road level. Approaching Kinloch Rannoch we had stopped briefly for a look at a throng of feeding greylags, an army so close-marshalled that in their field there seemed to be standing room only. Along the

side of Loch Rannoch the shadowed pines and birches of the Black Wood were snow-free, a recurrent pattern of moss-green and mulberry.

From Camghouran the first section of our round, up to the loch, was fractionally less than a mile and a half, a pleasant 30 minutes after a picnic lunch just off the main road. Some *larachan* beside the burn — cottage ruins huddled together barely above ground level — put us in mind of the village days long past. Then we were into a scattering of birches, looking down into a deepening gorge. Small falls linked brown and gold trout pools — far different from what we were to see on a later visit when the high snowfields were melting: a staircase of explosive linns giving one itchy feet to be doing a wet-suited gorge walk. Along the banks and beside our track, grotesquely twisted Scots pines were constant attractions, each more photogenic than the one before against the background blue of the sky. Then for a short spell we climbed away from the burn to a different pattern — tawny "lion grass" and chocolate heather clumps, with more birches, their bare winter branches the colour of over-ripe plums. A level stretch followed, where the puddles and the fringes of the burn were fretted with ice. And so out to open moorland, with big hills a far-off background to the south, a rampart looking twice its height, vague against the sun like a fake postcard photograph.

Had we been so minded, we might have followed the track for another five miles deep into the heart of these hills. Most remote among them is Meall Buidhe (3054 feet), a twin-topped Munro, the "yellow lumpy hill". More easily reached from the south, it gave a morning's enjoyment to my friend Theo Nicholson and myself one day of early December nearly 40 years ago. We approached it from Loch Giorra, a little loch up from Glen Lyon which disappeared later off the face of the map when hydro-electric progress merged it with its near neighbour Loch an Daimh. Showers of powder snow assailed us as we climbed then and also later in the afternoon on Stuchd an Lochain across on the south side of the loch, and we were glad of the light of a half moon to see us over the final moorland mile.

On our more prosaic walk from Camghouran we parted company with the main burn and its song at the edge of a stretch of level open country bordered on the far side by some fine stands of pines. We turned off westwards at a bridge over a diminutive side tributary curling in from Loch Monaghan. (It seemed more than a little ludicrous that this insignificant bridge on the road to nowhere should be dignified with the notice: "Warning — maximum load 38 tonnes gross.") The path here was muddy and unpromising, and we decided that the sheep which had been using it must have been few and far between. It was less than half a mile to the loch, which had only a thin ice-skin, particularly fragile-looking compared with the rock-hard sheet of our previous visit. There was no temptation to try conclusions with it.

The next section of the walk — another mile and a half — was virtually trackless. Now and again it did look as though one or two of the sheep had made half-hearted attempts to be public-spirited by treading out a wisp of path, but for the most part it was welly-boot work in damp moor-grass and heather. I wondered idly if any summer visitors might be tempted here to break into a stave or two of *The Road to the Isles* — "By heather tracks wi' heaven in their wiles." So far as we were concerned, the temptation was not particularly hard to resist.

Yet near surroundings and far views were more than adequate compensation. The second loch, Loch Finnart, had more character than Loch Monaghan, with a cluster of birch-topped islets suggesting interesting bird-territory in early summer. Ahead, and so vague in the afternoon haze as to defy any accurate assessment of height, the Easains, snow-stippled, looked like the distant wall of the Oberland.

Beyond the loch we crossed the furrow of the Allt Madais and joined a tractor track, not unlike a Wade road, but with more bends than would have pleased the General. This obviously led back down to Loch Rannoch and civilisation. It was a pleasant change from the tedium of heather tussocks, and we made good time downhill: to be precise, 17 minutes to the main road. The views ahead were now to the unmistakable snow-plateau of Ben Alder.

Down by the loch there was still a fair amount of sun-sparkle, but although it was only three o'clock it was not long before the January daylight began to fade. There was no mistaking the promise of another night of frost, with the clear sky steel-blue and, as we entered deeper shadow, with an arctic drop in temperature. Out in one or two of the inlets we could hear the occasional cracking of the ice-skin; soon it would be firming up as darkness fell. Yet the sun still played on the far shore of the loch in bright sequences of colour. In front we glimpsed now and again as we walked the polar tip of Schiehallion, and as if to add a further arctic touch, a quartet of whooper swans, calling hauntingly, passed in immaculate line ahead above the darkening lochside woods.

We were not minded to dawdle over this stretch of the 5½-mile round, and were soon enjoying the luxury of the car. We had been away just 2¾ hours. A winter round with an undoubtedly high star rating.

A PERTHSHIRE HILL with not even remote pretensions to "Munro" status, Ben A'an has nevertheless any amount of character to make up for its modest 1750 feet. Westwards it looks boldly across to Ben Venue over the deep bluffs of the Trossachs; its south face has the clean-cut symmetry of a cathedral spire, with a range of a dozen and more short rock-climbing routes, pleasantly varied in difficulty; from its summit far views reach up the eight-mile curve of Loch Katrine to a background semi-circle of familiar hills. Enough enjoyment and to spare to fill the longest evening in June.

It was, in fact, the last day of October when three of us paid what was for each a return visit. Accompanying Mais and me, our friend Joyce Watson had previously climbed the hill and dropped down the far side to the loch — a crossover we planned to imitate, with the walk back along the road from the Silver Strand the final leg of a 4½-mile round.

It was a day in a thousand to remember: on the way over from Aberfeldy, fresh snow, sun-drenched, on the Glen Lyon tops; Ben Lawers a final Everest pyramid, thin shreds of mist trailing across into background blue; moor grass and bracken and trees everywhere a breath-catching mix of autumn colours.

As we left the small car-park near the Trossachs (now Tigh Mhor) Hotel, the time was further into the afternoon than we would have liked; but the sun still shone, there was no wind to nag us, and the signposted path leading uphill from the road had an encouragingly easy tilt.

Away back in 1825, the author of *The Scottish Tourist*, writing at some length of the Trossachs, gave his imagination free rein when he came to describe Ben A'an:

North-east of Benvenue, and distant about a mile and a half, Ben-an lifts his white top 1800 feet above the level of the sea, a perfect pinnacle, and for the last 400 or 500 feet apparently inaccessible. In his ample sides, are dingle and bushy dell. Though his crest is cleft with lightning, he listens to the "crash of thunder, and the warring winds," without dismay; and, exposing his bare forehead to the tempest's shock, grimly guards the pass, "like a veteran gray in arms."

Needless to say, our own approach lacked any such high drama. Climbing between the edge of a wood and a field of "lion grass", the path took us on through the wood itself over a rich carpet of larch needles to the bank of the deep-cut burn. More level ground, tiresomely boggy, then saw us out to sunshine and an open stretch through deep bordering bracken. Hereabouts, as one writer has put it, "there are many little glades perfectly contrived for peaceful camp-

sites, and well sheltered from northern winds." Hereabouts, too, the way leads round to the rock-face where the climbs are to be found — routes first pioneered towards the end of last century by such "giants" of early Scottish climbing as W.W.Naismith and Harold Raeburn.

The easy angle of our own upward progress was too good to last. It steepened to an awkward stairway: large rocks, clearly positioned by an admirer of the builder of the Great Pyramid of Cheops, spaced so far apart that each upward step had to be a heave and a jerk. Fortunately this penance was not too long-lived and the blocks gave way to the kindlier angularities of a stream-bed. This duly petered out in more mud patches, with a snake-turn or two of path leading leftward to the actual summit of the Ben.

Joyce was off to the top crags, clearly hoping for a photograph or two before the westering sun was finally off the loch. Mais and I chose the easier option of continuing more sedately to the saddle of moor directly ahead. From here, if prospects looked encouraging, we would drop down to the woods and the road.

Summit or no, we had a grandstand view. The sun was still catching the tops of the distant

Winter walk among the pines above Camghouran.

peaks, a jumble of gold-tinted snow dustings, black-edged, with our point of reference to the extreme left — the triple prongs of The Cobbler. The latter gave the key to the pattern of all the Arrochar Alps and these in turn took us past Troisgeach ("Trotsky" of bygone Inverarnan days) to the Crianlarich group, most imposing of all the upper 1500 feet of Stobinian's long south ridge.

The silver S-bend of the loch itself brought back memories of a long day's walk starting in Glen Falloch below the Beinn Ghlas falls, crossing the watershed of Scotland over the grassy approaches to Beinn Chabhair, and descending Rob Roy's Glen Gyle to the road along the loch's edge — and the biggest blisters I have ever achieved. It had been autumn then, too, and the gold and flame of bracken and trees, reflected in the mirror-smooth water, have remained vividly bright pictures over the years.

There was no downhill track for us such as we had followed on the way up, but the eye of faith picked out a wisp of path obviously made by a few delicately treading sheep. This took us down through heather, home of a trio of protesting red grouse, to a fence and the first of a succession of steep, muddy banks, merging into a seemingly endless monotony of linked mudslides. We were still on a path of sorts, but slippery enough here and there to make us glad to have the fence or an occasional branch to hang on to. This second half of what we had hoped would be a complete walker's walk would no doubt be tolerable and even enjoyable in dry, summery conditions. We found it irksome and kept wondering often enough whether indeed we would ever see the road. Now and again we heard parties of tits and goldcrests in the trees, and somewhere overhead a raven provided a brief bass accompaniment; otherwise, there was not even a breeze stirring.

As we paused briefly after our slide through the wood, the road felt agreeably firm. The sun was down behind Ben Venue but the loch, unruffled round the black masses of the islands, mirrored the sky in bands of pinks and purples, hues a little less brilliant than that of Scott's Loch Katrine sunset in *The Lady of the Lake*,

> . . . gleaming with the setting sun,
> One burnish'd sheet of living gold,
> Loch Katrine lay beneath him roll'd.

It was all very peaceful, and we enjoyed our walk round the succession of inlets to the familiar end of the loch. The second mile through the Trossachs to the car-park and car was almost shadowy enough in the gloaming for us to appreciate the fanciful description again in the old tourist guide:

> Here the fox has his cover, and birds sit mute and motionless on the topmost bough, while the adder rears his obscene crest above the deadly nightshade. There a dreadful precipice frowns, and the beetling cliff projects horror over the dark ravine, "which even imagination fears to tread."

Happily we were able to negotiate the awesome pass without misadventure and reached the car unscathed, to enjoy the sight of an enormous, almost full October moon climbing over the silhouetted birches fringing the shore of Loch Achray.

Once Before

About Christmas-time we would go there
By the back roads, with fields of geese and a grey snow.
It was flat land, tousled in autumn with red clusters
And long stretches of poplar. The old couple
Were hewn from ash and the blown-down tree of a lost age.
They sat behind windows of blue-cold cloud
Welcomed us with fire and tea, green rooms of holly.
And he would take goose quills in his frayed grasp
Skill ink pens with a knife and tut his pipe.
There would be talk and a looking at old things
The clock in the hall and the skates with their many winters
Curled asleep in a box. Then the dark came
With frost of rough gemstones, the air pinched
With stars and balloons of breath. We had to go
That year and the year that came after
And now I don't know the way back.

INDEX

Aberfeldy, 18, 31, 41, 47, 48, 50, 51, 57
Aberfeldy Ferry, 65
Acharn, 78, 79, 85, 87
Acharn Fall, 79, 88
Amulree, 55, 60, 61, 63, 67, 85
Aspens, 48

Balrobbie Reserve, 37, 43, 44
Barvick Falls, 72, 73
Bedford Bridge, 92
Beich Falls, 77, 78
Beinn Chabhair, 9, 96
Beinn Chaluim, 9
Beinn a'Chroin, 9
Beinn Ghlas, 13, 16, 96
Beinn a'Ghlo, 15, 19, 43, 64
Beinn Laoigh, 11, 12
Beinn Tulaichean, 9, 11
Ben A'an, 94, 95
Ben Chonzie, 14, 15, 17, 18, 72
Ben Lawers, 9, 12, 15, 16, 85
Ben Ledi, 15, 77
Ben Lomond, 15
Ben More, 9, 15
Ben Nevis, 13, 15, 16
Ben Venue, 15, 42, 94, 95
Ben Voirlich, 14, 18, 60, 77
Ben Vrackie, 18, 19
Birks of Aberfeldy, 75
Birnam Oak, 50
Black Wood of Rannoch, 27, 54, 55, 56, 93
Blair Atholl, 91
Blair Castle, 19, 79, 81
Blairgowrie, 38
Bracklinn Falls, 73, 77
Bridge of Balgie, 29, 31
Bruar Falls, 79, 81
Bruarfoss, 81
Buchanty, 31, 33, 73
Burns, Robert, 75, 79
Burt, Edward, 59, 60, 61

Cairngorm Club, 17
Cairnwell, The, 19, 20
Callander, 42, 76, 77
Camghouran, 93
Campbell, Iain, 21, 25, 26, 31
Capercaillie, 45, 90
Carie, 27
Carn a'Chlamain, 19, 91, 92
Carn Liath, 19
Carn Mairg, 12, 61, 64, 73

Cassidy, Bob, 29
Chapman, Jim, 51
Charlie, Prince, 50, 55, 60, 62, 66
Clach Ossian, 61
Cochill Burn, 64
Cope, Sir John, 66
Corrymuckloch, 61
Coshieville, 26, 29, 36, 67, 73
Craigvinean Forest, 53, 85
Crianlarich, 9, 11, 30, 83
Crieff, 17, 40, 41, 59, 61, 63, 79
Cruach Ardrain, 9, 11
Culloden, 48, 59, 93
Cumberland, Duke of, 66

Dalnacardoch, 59, 62, 68
Dalnaspidal, 21, 27, 33, 69
Dowally, 89
Drever, Alan, 57
Drummond Hill, 36, 41, 45, 85, 87
Duinish, 25
Dunalastair, 36, 37
Dunkeld, 44, 50, 51, 52, 53, 68

Eagle, Golden, 85

Farragon, 18, 19, 47, 64, 76
Fender Burn, 63
Fendoch Burn, 60
Flycatcher, pied, 43
Flycatcher, spotted, 42
Forestry Commission, 48, 52, 55, 56
Fortingall, 12, 49, 50
Foulford Inn, 60, 74

Gilbert's Bridge, 91, 92
Glen Almond, 61, 85
Glen Falloch, 9, 12, 82
Glen Gyle, 85, 96
Glen Lochay, 29, 30
Glen Lyon, 12, 27, 29, 61, 78
Glen Quaich, 78, 79, 85
Glen Tilt, 19, 91, 92
Glengoulandie, 26, 37, 67
Glenshee, 20
Godwin, Gunnar, 52, 53
Gordon, Seton, 18, 50
Great Triangulation, 15, 16
Heart Wood, 47, 48
Hermitage, 52, 79
Humble Bumble, 76

Iceland, 37, 81
Innerwick, 27
Inverarnan, 9, 85, 96
Invergowrie, 41

Johns, Rev. C.A., 40, 42

Kearton, Richard, 40, 41
Keltie Falls, 72, 73
Keltie Water, 73, 74, 76
Keltney Burn, 26, 36, 67, 73
Kenknock, 30
Kenmore, 16, 39, 43, 78, 79, 87
Killiecrankie, 37, 41, 43, 44, 69
Killin, 13, 16, 30, 31
Kinloch Rannoch, 21, 23, 24, 25, 26, 36, 37, 67
Kiplonie Bridge, 72, 73

Lairig Chalbhath, 27, 28
Lairig nan Lunn, 29, 30
Larches, 51, 52
Leny, Falls of, 77
Little Glenshee, 32, 33
Loch Achray, 96
Loch na Craige, 31, 64
Loch an Daimh, 26, 36, 37
Loch Earn, 78
Loch Ericht, 24, 56
Loch Finnart, 94
Loch Freuchie, 40, 61, 85
Loch Garry, 21, 24, 33
Loch Katrine, 42, 83, 85, 94
Loch Kennard, 32, 43
Loch Kinardochy, 26, 36, 67
Loch Laidon, 39
Loch Lomond, 13, 42
Loch of the Lowes, 41, 89
Loch Lyon, 29
Loch Meallbrodden, 37, 38
Loch Monaghan, 93, 94
Loch Ordie, 42, 89
Loch Rannoch, 21, 27, 55, 56, 68, 93, 94
Loch Rotmell, 89
Loch Tay, 16, 31, 78, 85
Loch Turret, 17, 41, 72, 85
Lochay, Falls of, 31
Lubreoch, 29
Lurg Burn, 61

Macculloch, Dr John, 15, 16
Macdonald, Jim, 28, 29
Macmillan, Tavish, 54, 55
McNab, Andrew, 63

Meall Greigh, 85
Meall nan Tairneachan, 47
Meikleour, 44, 48

Menzies, Archibald, 49
Mill Dam, 42, 89, 90
Mitchell, Pat, 26, 27
Monzie, 72, 73, 74, 75
Moness Falls, 75, 76, 79
Munros, 15, 19, 20, 35, 39

Naismith, W.W., 16, 95
Newton Bridge, 61, 85

Ospreys, 41

Parent Larch, 51
Pennant, Thomas, 49, 76, 91, 92
Perth, 18, 36, 37, 76
Perthshire Mountain Club, 17, 18
Postbus, 28, 29

Rannoch Moor, 15, 29, 39, 85, 93
River Almond, 60, 61, 73
River Braan, 32, 52, 62
River Lyon, 74
River Tay, 20, 36, 37, 51, 55, 65
River Tilt, 79, 92

Schiehallion, 15, 18, 26, 67, 68, 73
Scottish Mountaineering Club, 16, 17
Scottish Tourist, The, 18, 79, 80, 92, 95
Shaggie Burn, 74, 75
Sma' Glen, 37, 43, 60
Statistical Account, 12, 13, 16, 18, 41, 42, 51, 52, 73, 75, 77, 92
Stobinian, 9, 96
Stormont Loch, 38
Strawberry Tree, 48, 49
Stuc a'Chroin, 14, 18, 60, 77
Swifts, 40

Trossachs, 83, 94, 96
Tummel Bridge, 36, 37
Turret Falls, 72, 73

Victoria, Queen, 19, 81, 89, 91, 92

Watson, Joyce, 94, 95
Watson, Professor W.J., 18, 92
Weem Inn, 48, 66, 67
Weem Rock, 40, 43, 48
Whooper swans, 26, 36, 37
Woodcock, 40, 73
Woodpecker, green, 40, 41
Wordsworth, William, 81, 82

Yew Tree, 49, 50